DON'T FEAR
THE GIG WORKER

DON'T FEAR
THE GIG WORKER:

GigCX And The Employment Reboot

by

Brian Pritchard,
Terry Rybolt,
and Mark Hillary

Don't Fear The Gig Worker:
GigCX And The Employment Reboot

© Brian Pritchard, Terry Rybolt, and Mark Hillary 2022
All Rights Reserved

Published by LiveXchange Books
Arroyo Grande, California, USA

https://livexchange.com
http://j.mp/gigcx

LiveXchange Books
1375 East Grand Ave, Suite 103 #238
Arroyo Grande,
California 93420
USA

Author portraits all supplied by the authors.

Cover by: Giovanni Misagrande

ISBN: 979-8-782-45926-0

Don't Fear The Gig Worker:
GigCX And The Employment Reboot
© Brian Pritchard, Terry Rybolt, and Mark Hillary 2022

This book is dedicated to the executives and managers who gave GigCX a chance in 2021– they realized that flexibility can be equally desirable for both workers and the companies they work for. The fourth industrial revolution is finally arriving...

CONTENTS

ABOUT THE AUTHORS

Brian Pritchard, is based in Toronto, Ontario, Canada and is the CEO of LiveXchange. A self-confessed entrepreneurial zealot and fully experienced in the difficult task of bringing new business ideas to successful operational fruition in challenging environments. Brian founded LiveXchange in 2002, long before work at home and gig economy were household terms. One of Brian's key strengths is in leading the cultural and technological changes as a corporation goes remote helping to change and advance the relationship between the corporation and the employee.

http://bit.ly/bpritchard
https://livexchange.com

Terry **Rybolt**, a 20 year BPO industry veteran, is the Chief Revenue Officer for LiveXchange based in Boston, MA, USA. Terry joined LiveXchange in 2020 after 12 years at Teleperformance serving in numerous executive functions, most recently as Managing Director, overseeing the global work at home go to market strategy for the company.

http://bit.ly/rybolt
https://livexchange.com

Mark **Hillary** is a British technology writer and analyst, based in São Paulo, Brazil. He studied Software Engineering and has an MBA from the University of Liverpool.

Mark co-hosts the CX Files podcast with CX analyst Peter Ryan–a weekly show focused on the future of customer experience. He frequently contributes to the global media, focused on technology and CX, with articles published by the BBC, Financial Times, Reuters, and Huffington Post. He has regular CX-focused columns in Intelligent Sourcing and Engage Customer.

Mark has written several books focused on technology. His first was titled 'Outsourcing to India: The Offshore Advantage' published in 2004 by Springer in Germany. He co-wrote 'Global Services: Moving To A Level Playing Field' with Dr Richard Sykes in 2007 for the British Computer Society and he translated all of Shakespeare's sonnets into tweets for his 2015 book 'My Tweets Are Nothing Like The Sun: William Shakespeare On Twitter.'

Mark has advised several national governments on technology policies and has advised the United Nations on the use of technology for development. He even co-authored a book titled 'Leveraging Social Media for SMEs' in 2013, published by the International Trade Center at the UN.

Brian, Terry, and Mark collaborated on a book titled 'GigCX: Customer Service in the Twenty-First Century.' Published in October 2020, this was the first published guide to GigCX. You can find a copy here: http://j.mp/gigcx

http://bit.ly/markhillary
http://carnabysp.com
Social: @markhillary

FOREWORD

> "Hold to the now, the here, through which all future plunges to the past."
>
> James Joyce, ULYSSES, 1922

When James Joyce wrote those words, the world was changing in what must have seemed unfathomable ways. And by the time he published FINNEGANS WAKE in 1939, there's a definite sense that Joyce felt everything was going too fast.

How many pints have Mark Hillary and I shared in pubs all over the world as we analyzed Joyce's perspicacious vision? Mark is somebody who gets it (I haven't met too many people who've read as much Joyce – as well as Joyce-obsessed Anthony Burgess – as I have).

He gets that we live in a world where change is constant and technology is accelerating us forward at fever-pitch. This is our "The Exponential Age." Such was the case before the Covid-19 pandemic, but since around March, 2020, the alien nature of societies in lockdown seems to have triggered a wave of events that are impacting us in ways that can never be reversed. It's a Joycean sense of vertigo. It's the "Fourth Industrial Revolution," squared. Don't believe me? The metaverse is soon to become a reality. Customers are constantly interacting with brands through an ambient customer experience process–smart speakers are always ready to respond to every request. The relationship between people and the brands they choose to purchase from has never been more complex, but this also makes the situation more interesting.

How can we imagine the world in five years, let alone a century? Looking back only a decade reveals a world before social media had flooded our world with fake news and vitriol. Where political leadership involved managing the economy, rather than just shaming the opposition. Where shopping usually involved shops. Where brands sold products and only communicated with customers to sell more, or to handle complaints.

Now I can have an ongoing relationship with my local grocery store. They send recipes and advice. They answer questions and reply with memes. Over 2 million people follow Dunkin' Donuts on Instagram to see cute photos of dogs with their nose inside a Dunkin' cup. One click and you can be wearing the t-shirt. America Runs on Dunkin' after all, especially in Boston.

Can you sense my enthusiasm for a hot cup of Dunkin'? For my beloved City on a Hill? Well, that's as it should be, no? In today's world, customers are now fans. We're no longer measuring interactions between customers and brands in the minutes it takes for a phone call to take place. There is now a lifetime of interaction.

The management of Domino's Pizza once told their employees to always imagine the customer has a $10,000 bill taped on their face. That's the value of that customer to us over the many years they will keep ordering our pizza. If they have a problem, and it might cost a few dollars to resolve, then fix it. We can lose a few bucks today because we want to earn all of that $10,000 over time.

There's much wisdom there, and the world is changing so quickly that Domino's management might need to also consider whether cryptocurrencies will soon become useful for everyday transactions. Will most customers someday use cryptocurrency to pay for their pizza? Either way, according to the U.S. Federal Reserve, the percentage of Americans preferring to pay with cash plunged from 27% in 2016 to 18% in 2020. The pandemic is no doubt accelerating that process.

Meantime, the process of managing customer interactions is maturing and can no longer be solely focused on the post-purchase phone call. People are interacting with brands they have never purchased from, building a relationship, and staying in touch with the brands they love. The entire process of managing the experience of a customer with a brand has evolved far beyond the concept of a contact center just managing calls.

What Brian, Terry, and Mark have illustrated in this book is that there is far more to GigCX than just the process of paying someone each time they help a customer–rather than paying an hourly wage.

The book indicates that there is a wider societal shift taking place. Our expectation of employers has changed. Workers no longer believe that commuting should just be accepted as essential or that an employer can deny them the flexibility to leave work early when they have a family emergency. The great resignation of 2021 indicated that millions of people are not prepared to skew their work/life balance entirely in favor of work. We all need to work, we have bills to pay, but we don't need to work in a way that destroys our physical and mental health.

GigCX is a result of many factors. The pandemic proved that professional employees could successfully work from home without a loss of productivity. I wrote about this over a decade ago, but it took a crisis for many executives to be convinced. Well, welcome to the future.

The widespread adoption of working from home has created the ability to introduce more flexibility into working hours. The continuous eight-hour shift was a result of the First Industrial Revolution. Factory employees were usually forced to spend long arduous hours at work and the agreement to limit shifts to just eight hours protected their health.

But in 2022, why is the Monday-Friday eight-hour shift still accepted as normal? We have workforce management software that can match up when companies need people and when people want to work. It should be simple to accommodate employees that want to do a few hours in the morning, then take a break to collect their kids from school, and then add in a couple more hours in the evening.

The gig economy has many critics, and often for a good reason, but GigCX is very different to the gig worker delivering restaurant meals. GigCX workers are choosing the brands they want to work for, how many hours they want to work, and when they want to work. GigCX agents are often fans of the brands they support.

Much of the debate around the great resignation has focused on the need for companies to listen to their workforce. To modernize and offer flexible hours and the ability to work from home when it is the preference of the worker. Companies that want to thrive in the 2020s need to pay more than just lip service to these requests for flexibility.

In fact, companies that offer their workers genuine flexibility will find that they are more attractive employers–so the best talent will gravitate in their direction. In addition, this ability to place workforce agility at the heart of operational strategy increases the resilience of the company to endure a future crisis–such as a new virus or disease that requires social distancing. Hopefully not in the near future though.

The doctrine of Milton Friedman is that a business is responsible only to the shareholders. This may need revision for the twenty-first century because a company that offers greater flexibility to its workforce will also create a more resilient organization that is ready for future challenges.

Listening to the workers may in fact also be better for the shareholders. And in the customer service environment it's likely that GigCX will be an increasingly popular organizational structure, not because it reduces operational cost, but because it's where the best talent can be located.

Far-sighted executives with one eye on the future need to chart a course that increases the resilience of their business and delivers the employee experience workers expect in the 2020s. GigCX has the potential to redraw how customer service strategies are designed and this book goes a long way to explaining why. All the future will soon plunge to the past. Don't get left behind. Cheers.

Stephen Loynd
Founder & Principal Analyst
TrendzOwl
Arlington, VA, USA
January 4, 2022
www.trendzowl.com
www.linkedin.com/in/stephenloynd/

PREFACE AND INTRODUCTION

> **"The great resignation is coming..."**
>
> ANTHONY KLOTZ
> Associate Professor of Management
> at Texas A&M University
> May 21, 2021 Bloomberg Businessweek

A lot has happened since our book 'GigCX: Customer Service In The Twenty-First Century' was published just over a year ago. When we sent the final draft of the book for publication it was still a week before Pfizer and BioNTech announced that their Covid-19 vaccine trial was successful.[1]

It still feels so recent, but at the time that book was published, there was still no vaccine and a large proportion of the world was living under lockdown conditions. Much has changed in 2021, but the path to a post-Covid society has been more challenging than anyone could have imagined at the end of 2020. Progressing to a 'new normal' is proving to be a very long and winding road.

But despite the challenges, we are getting there. The world is learning how to live and function again. But this experience has changed consumer behavior and attitudes. At the time we are writing this introduction, the Covid-19 pandemic has killed over 5.5 million people. Almost 300 million have contracted the virus. Millions of people have witnessed illness and death up close.

In the middle of 2021 it was fairly common to read about more than a million Americans quitting their job every week. Anthony Klotz coined the term 'the great resignation' and a media storm continued for months as experts and analysts all asked why so many people are quitting–often not even changing job.

The Harvard Business Review analyzed over 9 million employee records at over 4,000 companies and summarized two main causes for the great resignation:[2]

1. With more people working from home (WFH), mid-career professionals with employee experience are far more attractive than younger employees that need more in-person coaching. So the market for mid-career professionals exploded.

2. Many mid-level professionals will have avoided changing job during the pandemic, so as restrictions eased there was a double-whammy of more people looking for jobs and better offers.

Anthony Klotz and several other labor experts have suggested that the 'carpe diem' effect was also a major factor in accelerating the situation. This is where people question the value of their occupation and decide on a change of direction in their life. Why am I doing this when I don't even enjoy it? I'm outta here!

Whatever the reason, companies were losing people. Some HR leaders suggested that smart companies could turn this situation to their advantage. By reviewing what their employees want from work and responding quickly to suggestions, some companies could potentially turn the great resignation into the great attraction.[3]

The lesson here is that workers wanted more flexibility in their work location and working hours. Some wanted to return to offices, but many preferred to stay working from home. Workers, in general, wanted employers to acknowledge that they had delivered throughout the challenge of the pandemic–maybe they could start asking for the right to work from home and expect a little more flexibility over their hours?

Academics proved the value of working from home several years ago. Perhaps the best known study was by Professor Nicholas Bloom of Stanford University. Bloom led an experiment with the Chinese travel agency CTrip in 2013 and demonstrated a 13% increase in performance for customer service agents working from home. In addition, home-based workers took fewer breaks and days off sick. The productivity gain of working from home was similar to every employee doing an extra day of work every week.[4]

Some analysts are now asking if offices add any value at all when home-based professionals are so much more productive.[5] The loudest voices crying out for a full-time return to offices are often commercial landlords or the owners of city center coffee stores.

We know the world has changed. Even those companies that retain offices are now offering their employees greater location flexibility.[6] Major city centers are now far quieter on Monday and Friday as office workers focus their in-person meetings in the middle of the week.

Contact centers are no exception. When 5th Talent talked to almost 6,000 contact center workers in 13 different countries in 2021 they found that only 2% of the workers wanted to return to working in a contact center 100% of the time.[7]

This book aims to explore this problem. Managers responsible for customer service processes know that their team wants more flexibility, but just allowing people to work from home is not the complete answer. If you need to work from 9am until 6pm every single day with a remote boss telling you when breaks are allowed then that isn't very flexible–even if the worker no longer has to commute to an office.

The pandemic proved that WFH works. Academics like Nicholas Bloom had been publishing about this several years earlier. Our foreword author, Stephen Loynd, can point to his own published research from 15+ years ago promoting the virtues of WFH.

But real flexibility is about more than just the location where work is performed–for both employer and employee. Look at this summary from December 2021 of the four main challenges facing contact centers in 2022:[8]

1. Reducing waiting times
2. Continuing to engage with remote workers
3. Recruitment and retention
4. Low customer satisfaction

These are perennial problems. If your contact center is making customers wait, customers hate the service they receive, you aren't comfortable allowing WFH to continue, and you can't find anyone who wants to work in your company then your current methods are not working.

In September 2021, the most in-demand job in the US was customer service representative.[9] People want these jobs in customer service, but we all know that contact centers traditionally face attrition rates that are over 100%. That's right, it's typical to change every single person in the company every year.

There is another way to offer flexibility to employees and to build a bench of flexible talent for employers. In the customer service industry we call this GigCX.

Our earlier book introduced and explained the concept, but we want to go further now, to explore why employees are now demanding greater flexibility and what employers can do to meet these demands in a way that creates a win-win situation.

GigCX is focused on finding great talent and then engaging these people in a flexible way. The company indicates when it needs people and the workers match up the times when they want to work with the company needs. The workers are usually paid for each customer that is assisted–not for the time they spend on the job.

This can feel unsettling for anyone used to the concept of being paid to work by the hour. Government minimum wage standards are entirely based on the principle that workers are paid by the hour, not by their actions or achievements.

But in many industries this focus on delivery has been accepted for many years. There are still some journalists that receive a fixed monthly salary, but most are paid for each article they write.

As the authors of this book and our earlier effort to explain GigCX, we have often wondered if GigCX is the right title for this employment structure. When gig is mentioned, most people think of restaurant delivery drivers–paid for each delivery and working long grueling days just to achieve a low income.

GigCX differs in many ways. GigCX workers choose the brands they want to work with. They are often fans of the brands they choose to support. GigCX workers can almost always earn much more than their peers working inside a contact center on a salary–payment for helping each customer is more valuable than a fixed hourly rate.

Employers that require flexibility at different times, such as the annual Black Friday boom in retail, can build a large bench of trained workers–many more than they usually require–so they can call on this pool of talent when needed. Everyone works from home so there is no need to worry about increasing the team by 50% for a month.

Many legislators, politicians, and even business leaders are still concerned about the gig economy. The Federal Trade Commission is working on various initiatives to restrict gig companies in the US and the European Union has drafted legislation granting employment rights–such as vacation time–to gig workers.[10, 11]

GigCX is a very different proposition to restaurant meal deliveries and in this book we will attempt to describe how a traditional customer service strategy–captive and internal or via an outsourced supplier–can be augmented with GigCX. The debate here is how GigCX can improve how customer service strategies function–not how we need to replace everything that currently exists with GigCX.

In this post-pandemic business environment it is very clear that companies require more agility and resilience than ever. Companies that survived the pandemic did so because they could quickly pivot and change focus. This requirement for agility will now be an ongoing requirement.

But employees also want change. They want to work from home when it suits them. They want to finish early to see their kid's school play. They want professional jobs with great opportunities for progression, but without the traditional need to be stuck in an office for long hours at least five days a week.

In the customer service industry GigCX offers a way forward. We are not just designing more flexible customer service solutions, we are demonstrating the future of work itself. Connect the dots from the pandemic move to WFH and the present-day demand for flexibility and GigCX looks like an important part of the solution.

This book is a series of short essays that explores how work in changing in the 2020s and how Gig CX will be an essential component for the future of designing customer service solutions–we hope you find it both useful and enjoyable!

Brian Pritchard
Terry Rybolt
Mark Hillary
January 10, 2022

INTRODUCTION REFERENCES:

1. https://www.pfizer.com/news/press-release/
   press-release-detail/pfizer-and-biontech-
   announce-vaccine-candidate-against
2. https://hbr.org/2021/09/
   who-is-driving-the-great-resignation
3. https://www.thehrdirector.com/
   great-resignation-become-great-retention/
4. https://www.gsb.stanford.edu/faculty-
   research/working-papers/does-working-
   home-work-evidence-chinese-experiment
5. https://www.npr.org/sections/coronavirus-
   live-updates/2021/11/09/1053793602/
   future-of-work-author-says-its-time-to-
   ask-if-offices-are-worth-it
6. https://www.forbes.com/sites/
   kristinstoller/2021/01/31/never-want-to-
   go-back-to-the-office-heres-where-you-
   should-work/?sh=23ecaad96712
7. https://www.5thtalent.com/
   work-at-home-study-april-2021
8. https://www.cmswire.com/customer-
   experience/4-of-the-top-call-center-
   challenges-for-the-coming-year
9. https://lensa.com/insights/the-lensa-index/
10. https://news.bloomberglaw.com/daily-
    labor-report/gig-economy-rise-prompts-
    ftc-chiefs-call-to-alter-antitrust-law
11. https://www.theguardian.com/business/2021/
    dec/09/gig-economy-workers-to-get-
    employee-rights-under-eu-proposals

CHAPTER ONE:

COULD THE GREAT RESIGNATION BE A GREAT OPPORTUNITY FOR YOUR BUSINESS?

A recent article[1] in The HR Director magazine suggested the American 'great resignation'[2] could become the 'great retention' or even the 'great attraction' for companies that actually listen to their employees during this uncertain period. Leaders that listen and take action to remodel their companies in a way that embraces flexibility can make the entire company more attractive–for the existing employees and for people searching for a new employer.

Here is a short section from the article:

"The opportunity is to listen to your employees and be proactive. Go and ask them what you can do to support them and to create a more flexible working environment. Find all the reasons for dissatisfaction and then take action. There has never been a more unusual time in our working lives so all ideas should be on the table – find out what your employees really want."

This is so true. If you are not going to take action now, after a global pandemic forced every office worker to work from home, then when are you going to start listening to what your employees want and need?

Critics of the great resignation argue that it's really just pent-up demand. All the people that were thinking about changing job in early 2020 are now taking action because they can see that the pandemic restrictions have eased and it's now possible to change employer.

That's a partial explanation, but we don't think this is the only reason. Since March 2020, many of us have been surrounded by illness and death. If we have not lost a friend or family member to Covid then we all know someone who was struck down and spent days in bed hoping it wasn't going to be serious. This has been a very unusual time. You need to look back to the Spanish flu a century ago for any comparable experience.

When you start looking around, there are many examples of people that have just had enough. Look at this cook in Alaska[3], tired of working long hours in hospitality for low pay. She took a coding boot camp and now has a job as a software engineer-better, more flexible hours, and better pay. Multiply that story a few million times and we think that you might have a closer idea of what is really happening.

Compensation is not the only factor. Paying people an extra 50 cents an hour will not keep them coming into jobs they don't enjoy. Employers need to be thinking more strategically-how do I offer more flexibility in a way that works for my business and also helps the employees to enjoy a better work/life balance?

The old feel-good statements about offering work-life balance are no longer enough. If you are forcing an employee to commute into the office when they asked for some flexibility because their child is sick then your business will not retain this expertise.

In our area of focus, customer service, we are already seeing a revolution taking place and Covid was the catalyst. When millions of contact center agents across the world had to work from home it was quickly proven that it was possible to make it work and to make it secure. Who really needs those aircraft hangar contact centers when we can do this differently?

Combine work from home with a GigCX approach that allows much more flexibility and you then create a customer service environment that's great for the employees and it also delivers flexibility for the business. You need flexibility over Black Friday? It's not a problem with GigCX.

As the HR Director article suggests, companies that enter 2022 with a more flexible approach–because they learned from the pandemic–are going to become attractive employers. Those that are just trying to 'return to normal' are going to struggle.

CHAPTER TWO:

DO 4-DAY WEEKS PROVE THAT MORE HOURS IS NOT MORE PRODUCTIVITY?

In many of Terry's articles here[1], he has focused on why GigCX is about so much more than just creating a flexible contact center. This is a different way of working that creates more flexibility for companies that want to manage seasonality, but critically this also addresses one of the most important job requirements for employees today-their own need for flexibility.

One of the key points we have been making throughout 2021 is that there needs to be less of a connection between time spent on a job and what is achieved. This has been a traditional problem in contact centers because customers often call in clusters-there can be really busy periods where a service agent is helping a new customer every couple of minutes and then there are times when they are just waiting for a call.

Regardless of what the agent is doing, they get the same pay per hour because almost every employer just pays an hourly rate-often close to the minimum wage if they feel they can. Those 8-hour shifts aren't really efficient.

But take a look[2] at what this European digital banking company, Atom Bank[3], is now doing in the UK. Atom Bank is a leading challenger bank in Europe and has 430 employees at their British head office so it's not a huge company, but it's also far from a startup with a dozen people in a WeWork. The CEO of Atom Bank, Mark Mullen, has announced that everyone in the company can work 34 hours over 4 working days, rather than 37.5 hours over 5 days. So the shifts on each day are slightly longer, but everyone gets a 3-day weekend. This change in working hours includes the c-suite–everyone in the company benefits and they believe that it will improve both wellbeing and employee retention.

Naturally, the Atom Bank employees need to coordinate their long weekends with other team members so there is always someone working, but it's clear that this is a company that is listening to what their employees want and taking action. "Before Covid, the conventional wisdom was you had to commute in, sit at a desk all day and repeat that process when you commuted home," said Mr Mullen.

Experiments like this are echoing what we saw many years ago with Henry Ford. Back then, it was normal to work six days a week and only have Sunday off. Ford believed that a two-day weekend would give his employees more leisure time (as Sunday was usually for church) therefore boosting both productivity and wellbeing.

Now employers are asking their employees, can you achieve just as much in 4 days as you can in 5 if we give you the support you need to improve efficiency and productivity? If so, take a three-day weekend.

There is a growing international movement of companies that are listening to their employees and trying their best to create a flexible work environment that genuinely offers the ability to create a more positive work/life balance.

In the customer service environment, GigCX is going to play an important role in 2022. It offers employers the flexibility to always manage seasonal peaks, but it also offers employees the ability to take days off when needed or to be there for a school parent's evening. As Mr Mullen of Atom Bank suggests, the days of working Monday to Friday in the same place with the same commute should be consigned to the history books.

Employers that want to succeed in the post-Covid flexible work environment need to embrace flexibility for employees and in the customer service environment this is going to mean embracing GigCX.

CHAPTER THREE:

CUSTOMER SERVICE REPRESENTATIVES ARE THE MOST IN-DEMAND WORKERS IN THE USA IN 2021

One of the most enduring news stories of 2021 has been the 'Great Resignation.' As workers move on from the pandemic, and start piecing together a post-pandemic work and home life, they have often found that they don't really like the way their career was going in 2019.

4.4 million Americans quit their job in September alone.[1] 4.3 million quit in August. There are many factors at play here, but what's clear is that this is highly unusual. A Washington Post story by Eli Rosenberg published on November 12 explained: "... workers have remained remarkably mobile, quitting jobs for a variety of reasons and often with little notice. Many businesses are so strapped to find and retain workers that they are dipping into budgets to offer higher pay and bonuses, creating the most worker-friendly labor market in recent history."

The jobseeker website Lensa recently published detailed research[2] on who is hiring in the US, where, and what they are offering. The research also included the most in-demand type of jobs in the US right now. The top 5 were:

1. Customer service representative
2. Receptionist
3. Administrative assistant
4. Customer service
5. Warehouse associate

Take a look at that list again. Two out of the top five most in-demand job positions in the US in 2021 are focused on customer service. So let's just focus on the number one position–the customer service representative.

What's a typical customer service position like? Usually it is paid at minimum wage, or close to it. It requires the employee to commute to an out of town contact center where they need to put in a full continuous shift of at least eight hours. It's intense, with few chances to rest once a shift begins.

It's quite a tough job to spend all day talking to customers that have a problem–many of them getting angry and upset because they want that problem resolved right now. Costco starting wages are now $17 per hour.[3] Starbucks is paying baristas from $15 to $23 an hour. Would you rather be serving coffee than working on a phone for eight hours a day?

There is nothing wrong about working in customer service, but the structure of traditional contact center jobs just doesn't match up to what people want or expect today. They want more flexibility and control over their working day. They want the ability to take a rest if they need it, or an afternoon off because they have family responsibilities.

Customer service representatives are the most in-demand jobs in the US at present, but so many companies are not exploring how to answer the doubts and uncertainties triggering the great resignation. These jobs need to evolve to meet the expectations of the people who could fill those positions.

GigCX offers a much more flexible work environment for customer service representatives. They can work from home, choose the hours they want to work, and get rewarded each time they help a customer. This is how customer service jobs would function if we designed them for the twenty-first century instead of just assuming that the huge contact centers are how this functions, because that's how it always worked in the past.

GigCX addresses the doubts and fears many workers demonstrated during the Great Resignation. It gives them more control. It gives them more flexibility. It allows them to take a day off, or to put in some extra hours. They can take back control over their working life and even choose the companies they are representing–so they can work on customer service for brands they actually care about.

GigCX also helps the companies that need to hire customer service representatives. Nobody cares if you offer an extra 50 cents an hour if the job still requires a commute to a business park and long inflexible hours. Turn that around. Offer your people more flexibility and watch your recruitment get easier and employee turnover stop overnight.

CHAPTER FOUR:

GIGCX CAN CHANGE THE DEBATE ABOUT THE FUTURE OF WORK

The Federal Trade Commission is pushing[1] to change US antitrust law so the current exemptions applied to traditional labor unions can be applied to gig economy workers. On the surface this looks like a typical gig economy story where workers that are fighting for higher pay, and better working conditions, find legal obstacles tossed in their way as they fight for greater fairness.

Many gig companies have been engaged in an endless back and forth push over the arguments about the rights that gig economy workers should expect. This is to be expected. Prop 22 in California[2] demonstrated that there are legal arguments on both sides of the debate that people will support. It's a battle at present.

But, we think that everyone should look beyond many of the present-day arguments and start considering the future of work itself. Mark once heard an employment professor say something like '...my father had one job throughout his entire career, I will have seven jobs in my career and my son will have seven jobs at the same time in his career.'

Regardless of the gig economy, our ideas around work and employment have been changing for a long time. Nobody thinks of a permanent job with a single employer as being literally 'permanent' today.

The FTC, the unions, Uber, and all these companies that are fighting over how work should be structured in 2021 are all basing their views on how work used to look. The workers want fixed hours, fixed pay, benefits, and a union to protect them. The employer wants greater flexibility and the freedom to change their plans if they need to take the business in a new direction.

We all know this. Even the FTC and their current action sounds ill-advised. Why use antitrust law to prevent gig workers claiming more rights? This approach to the law and the way we are structuring modern jobs isn't fit for purpose for workers and also for employers. We need to be fighting for fairness and opportunity.

Our focus is customer service, which is great because the most in-demand American workers in 2021 are customer service representatives.[3] Let's look at what companies need from their customer service representatives and what most representatives want.

- **Company requirement from representatives:** be knowledgeable, reliable, helpful, flexible, communicate well, put the customer at ease and create a good experience.
- **Representatives requirement from employers:** respect my knowledge, give me flexibility to choose my hours

and take time off when I need to, let me access my pay as I earn it, treat me as a valuable professional.

In a traditional customer service environment it usually feels like a war against the numbers. Many people apply for the jobs, but very few are accepted, and then many people quit as well, so it's a constant race. A typical contact center environment will replace every worker inside a year.

GigCX totally changes how the job is defined, rewarded, and the incentives for performing a customer service representative job.

- The agent can choose which brands they want to represent–so they only work for brands they actually care about. If you are into fashion then would you prefer to help fashion customers or life insurance customers? How does that impact on loyalty?
- The agent is rewarded for each customer helped.
- The agent can choose their hours.

What we are really doing with the GigCX environment is asking how work can be designed so it meets the flexible needs of the employer and also the demands for job flexibility that many employees are now demanding.

Your kids are in the school play so you need to finish early on Thursday? No problem. You need to take Friday off because you are planning a long family weekend? No problem. You want to work a bit extra for the next couple of weeks to save more for a vacation? No problem.

This is the kind of flexibility that modern workers are asking for and the GigCX concept helps workers gain this flexibility and gives employers the ability to also manage their own workforce strategy.

The gig economy argument is not about how to give gig workers union representation or which companies are not looking after their gig workers-we should not respond to the debate by using the tools of the past. We need to be designing high quality jobs that are fulfilling and exciting for the workers in a way that also creates the flexibility that companies need.

Let's change the debate and start designing the flexible jobs of the future. GigCX is a great start.

CHAPTER FIVE:

TALENT-AS-A-SERVICE BECOMES A REALITY AS FREELANCERS BECOME THE US MAJORITY

The workplace is changing. We know there is a large group of people who still believe that a job involves an office and a suit, but real-life isn't Mad Men.[1] The world really has changed. Over a third of all American workers are now freelance. If current trends continue then more than half of all Americans will be freelance by 2027.[2]

We are talking about a near future where a single job with a single employer expecting you to arrive at the same office and work the same hours each day will be an activity that only a minority of workers are engaged in.

The gig economy will allow more workers to benefit by selling their talent and being rewarded for what they actually deliver, rather than the number of hours spent sitting in a cubicle updating Facebook.

This isn't a radical view. Think about all the professionals that have been working this way for a long time. Journalists paid for each article they write. Graphic designers paid for each completed project. Coders building apps. Getting paid for what they do, rather than how long they are at work is normal in many professions, but with this rapid growth in freelancers it is soon going to be more common than an hourly wage.

The startup and small business magazine, YFS, recently published[3] a thought-provoking article about what they called 'Talent-as-a-Service.' Think about the situation where you are running a fast-growing startup and you need some SEO advice quickly–or you need some board level advice before taking a major decision.

These are regular jobs where you could advertise them and hire someone on a full-time basis–if you can find someone. They are also gigs. There are already platforms out there that allow you to appoint an SEO expert just for as long as they are needed.

Some board level executives are now using their trusted reputation to deliver services to multiple companies in a fractional way. An example might be an experienced Chief Marketing Officer who decides to offer their services charged by the day. They can have three or four clients and a long weekend every week.

Companies have always used part-time employees and day-rate contractors, but there is a changing dynamic here. Many of these opportunities are now defined as gigs, rather than a fixed period of time–so there is a project or task to be completed rather than a day spent in the office.

Organizations that start building their workflow around gigs are finding that they can achieve more by matching the work to the skilled worker, rather than believing that every single worker needs to be hired onto a payroll and employed for 40 hours a week–even if the tasks don't match the hours.

The growth in the number of freelancers in the US demonstrates this point. More and more workers want the flexibility of choosing their hours, choosing where they will work, choosing who they will work for, and choosing how much they want to work.

A fundamental change is taking in place in what it means to be employed. A job is no longer something you do in the same way each day for the same employer.

CHAPTER SIX:

HFS RESEARCH SAYS 'GET READY FOR GIG CX!'

Terry has been arguing right here[1] for months, maybe even longer, that Gig CX is about more than just BPO or contact centers. Gig CX is not replacing BPO, it is offering captive contact centers and BPOs the opportunity to create a genuinely flexible work environment. This is a fundamental change in how people work.

Some of the analysts are listening. Take look at this summary of Gig CX by Melissa O'Brien of HfS Research.[2]

Let's consider come of the key points that Melissa raises here:

- **Gig work has been around for a long time.** We don't need to keep looking at services like Uber when gig platforms like Upwork have been around for decades.
- **Gig CX is flexible** and allows existing BPOs to augment what they are doing.
- **Gig CX allows brands to tap into their fans-** you can find highly specialized expertise in

gig workers ... people who would never go for a job in a contact center.

Melissa's article summarizes Gig CX this way: "Operations leaders worth their salt must absolutely be exploring the potential for gig to augment their workforce." She added: "The pandemic has fueled a cultural shift. The idea of working from anywhere means you don't have to be tied to a desk, and gig is just the next phase of that shift. Enterprise operations leaders must examine this delivery option if they haven't already as a lever to pull for staff augmentation and improved CX."

Must absolutely be exploring... that's a strong statement. The team at HfS Research believes that the pandemic has changed how people work and what employees expect from employers. Gig CX can tap into a home-based labor pool that works flexible hours because that's exactly what they want from their job.

At last! Someone in the analyst community can see that Gig CX is actually good for the workers–they get the flexibility they are demanding. It's good for the employer–they also get the flexibility to scale their customer service operation up and down as required. It's also great for the customer because we don't want to hear excuses about Covid or Black Friday–we just want to be served efficiently.

Do take a few minutes to read Melissa's article because we believe the tide is turning. Gig CX is no longer a prediction for the future of customer service. It's right here, right now, and smart brands are already out there finding people who love their products and asking those fans if they want to work part-time helping other customers.

CHAPTER SEVEN:

CAN YOU SERVE ALL YOUR EXTRA CUSTOMERS IN THE POST-COVID BOOM?

The Covid-19 pandemic has been a disaster for many industries, but we are now seeing more than just the shoots of recovery–some sectors are soaring. Take a look at apparel sales for one example.[1] Compared to the same period (Q4) in 2019 analysts are expecting to see a 59% increase in sales this year.

That's compared to the last final quarter before the pandemic. The level of growth is astonishing. We expect that some of this growth is pent-up demand–customers spending less during the pandemic are returning again–but even so, it's still impressive.

Many of the new shopping behaviors we experienced during the pandemic will stick around as well. 18% of customers bought products online that they had only ever bought in-person before.[2] 35% said that they did not miss in-person shopping. 33% of millennials bought items from another country using e-commerce platforms–often purchasing directly from brands rather than retailers.

Retail companies often face problems when sales temporarily increase. How long have you had to wait in the past when trying to return a product bought during Black Friday or Cyber Monday? If many different retail sectors are facing a similar boom to apparel then customer service levels are going to deteriorate dramatically.

What's the answer?

This research by Upwork indicates a very good place to start.[3] There are around 60 million freelance workers in the USA alone-gig workers. They actively choose to get paid for individual tasks (gigs) rather than basing their income on the amount of hours or days worked.

This model applies for the customer service environment too. Retailers that are struggling to cope with a 59% increase in sales, and all the extra customer interactions this will inevitably create, need to tap into this pool of workers. You can't just ask everyone to wait while you build an extension to your contact center.

Use your contact center as the core of your customer service team, but build up a bench of workers hired using a "gig cx" model. Then you can ramp up quickly to cover the sales and holidays. You can reduce cover when it gets quiet again in January. You can expand your gig team without the need to build any additional facilities-these are all going to be agents working from home.

LiveXchange is a platform that allows you to keep and maintain your existing customer service team. You can use the platform to augment your existing team with a gig CX team. They can work together and alongside each other and seamlessly integrate into your existing processes.

Almost 60 million Americans are now working this way. They want flexibility and they want to be paid each time they help a customer. You should be enjoying this market growth, not struggling to serve everyone and developing a reputation as a brand that lets down loyal customers.

Keep your contact center, but build a flexible layer on top so you can tap into the millions of workers who actively want to operate within the gig economy.

CHAPTER EIGHT:

GIG CX OFFERS WHAT WORKERS WANT MOST—FLEXIBILITY

A new movie has been doing the rounds of the international festival circuit.[1] Titled 'The Gig Is Up' it explores the growing gig economy and asks what kind of regulation we need to introduce if gig work becomes more common than it already is.

We agree there is a need to revisit regulation and employment law. The current idea of 40-hours a week from Monday to Friday is rooted in the era of the industrial revolution. As we recover from the pandemic, companies are seeing increased demand from workers for more flexible work that allows them to manage their other commitments.

This is where the gig economy does actually have a strength that is often overlooked. It is naturally flexible. If you are getting paid for what you deliver, rather than the number of hours worked then you can work less one day and more the next day—or finish early because you need to collect your kids from school. Gig work is naturally flexible.

We haven't seen 'The Gig is Up' yet, but from the trailer it is clear that the central theme is that gig work often exploits workers. In one scene a gig worker points at a screen and says that the job on offer is paying one cent per gig–who would work for a cent?

This idea of a race to the bottom is a danger, but we need to explore how the flexible nature of gigs can be combined with more fulfilling and valuable work. What if the jobs that people liked could have gig elements to them–like being able to work more flexible hours?

This isn't just an aspiration. Look at the research undertaken by Harvard Business School where they analyzed data from over 400,000 food delivery drivers in California.[2] Most of us have used these services–DoorDash, Uber Eats, or Grubhub are all examples.

In the research, the riders valued their ability to flexibly control their working hours as having a cash value of about 17% of their earnings. To put that another way, if the company were to force them to work fixed hours then they believe a fair trade-off would be to reduce their working hours by approximately an entire day per week.

They really, really, value their flexibility.

But restaurant delivery isn't a very complex service. You don't need an advanced degree or specialist knowledge. You just need a bike and the desire to work hard. If workers in this fairly commoditized work environment are demanding greater flexibility and control over their hours, then what do you think other workers are expecting?

That's right–they want even more flexibility. In the customer service industry we have all known this for a long time. Attrition rates at most contact centers were terrible in 2019–often 100% of employees will be replaced inside a year.[3] Just imagine how attrition rates will be looking now that everyone has had a taste of life without a long commute and a boss staring over their shoulder. This is where we can leverage the gig economy to create flexible and fulfilling opportunities for people who want to work helping customers, but cannot commit to an eight-hour shift five days a week.

Gig CX is not about exploitation. It's about finding flexible experts that want to work from home. It's about finding people who want to help customers, but in a way that fits in with their lifestyle. Tens of millions of Americans are now choosing to work in this way. We can create gig economy opportunities that are both fulfilling and flexible–it's up to us in the industry to demonstrate that the gig economy can offer both well-paid and flexible opportunities.

CHAPTER NINE:

ENSURING YOUR WFH AGENTS ARE SECURE NEEDS MORE THAN JUST THIN CLIENTS

One of the most important differences between Gig CX and a traditional customer service operation is that all the agents are based at home. There is no need for a physical contact center. Nobody is commuting and working shifts in a contact center.

In the LiveXchange case, a contact center does exist, but it is a virtual contact center in the cloud. Customers connect to the center and it routes them to the agents at home. Naturally this means that the end-to-end security needs to be particularly strong.

This was a challenge for many companies at the start of the pandemic–not just those focused on customer service. Every company that asked their employees to work from home needed to deploy a new form of network security rapidly because instead of just protecting the network inside a physical office, suddenly the network was scattered across thousands of locations.

Many companies claim to have thin-client systems that allow remote workers to connect safely. There are some good solutions out there, but one of the biggest issues with almost all of the systems we have seen is that someone has to setup, install, and configure the security.

Imagine you have just onboarded a new employee and they are going to use their own device from home. Either that employee has to physically take the device to your office, so the IT team can configure it, or they need to allow the IT team to remotely access their device. We have witnessed some of these remote configuration sessions and they can go on for hours because everyone is using different devices from different manufacturers–there is no standardization.

Our LiveXchange system is very different. It's called SecureWorkSpace (SWS). The SWS software instantly transforms the agent's PC into a secure workstation. It uses a secure VPN to create a private connection to the client's network and all locally stored files and applications are blocked. The remote PC can be used, but only for the purpose of helping customers of the client the agent is working for.

This is a quote from one of our clients, commenting on the SWS solution: "LiveXchange's PCI technology identifies, isolates and secures agents and their desktops as they access the work environment. Each agent is issued a physical "secure OS token", which binds their identity to our server, bypasses their local OS, encrypts their connection and assures compliance – all in less than 60 seconds."[1]

That's the important point to note–60 seconds. It's secure, it sets itself up, and it can be configured in less than a minute. Now ask your colleagues with expertise in networking and security how long they have spent setting up remote devices over the past 18 months and we are sure that will sound even more impressive.

CHAPTER TEN:

HOW HAS THE GREAT RESIGNATION AFFECTED YOUR INDUSTRY?

The world is changing fast. The post-pandemic wave of resignations has been called the Great Attrition–or is it the Great Attraction or Great Resignation? A year and half after the start of this pandemic, many employees are asking if they really want to carry on doing the same thing day after day.

Of course most people need their job just to keep paying the bills, but expectations are genuinely changing. Look at this AP coverage of the high-end holiday tree manufacturer, Balsam Hill.[1] They recently lost 4 out of 5 employees at their new store in Dallas because the employees didn't want to work weekends. They were forced to close the store for weeks until new employees could be found. The difference this time is that the company has been working with each individual on their shift pattern– the workers are defining their working hours.

The most recent McKinsey Quarterly explored the issue in some depth.[2] McKinsey reports that over 19 million American workers quit their job from April to September 2021. The article explains: "If the past 18 months have taught us anything, it's that employees crave investment in the **human** aspects of work. Employees are tired, and many are grieving." The traditional transactional nature of work isn't working. Employers that think they can retain talent by paying an extra few cents an hour are about to get a very rude awakening. Employees want interactions, not just transactions. McKinsey warns that many executives do not understand this, the effect is accelerating, and many companies are at risk because of the management failure to adapt and learn.

What we keep on hearing in the news coverage of this "Great Resignation" is that workers are focusing more than ever on their own wellbeing.[3] Work-life balance used to be something that most people aspired to, but few achieved. Now the flexibility to really manage all aspects of a job and family life is becoming essential for many workers. They will not tolerate inflexibility from their employer.

Anthony Klotz, an organizational psychologist at Texas A&M University explained the great resignation this way: "During the pandemic, because there was a lot of death and illness and lockdowns, we really had the time and the motivation to sit back and say, do I like the trajectory of my life? Am I pursuing a life that brings me well-being?"

A recent article in Forbes by Jessica Lin demonstrates how work can change.[4] Lin describes a transformational approach to hiring customer service agents. Look at the traditional model, where a contact center employs agents to work fixed shift patterns and recruits people that appear to be friendly or helpful. Now contrast that to hiring people who love a specific brand and will actually enjoy helping customers. Imagine you love a specific fashion brand and you regularly post images on Instagram featuring their products. The company gets in touch to say: 'Hey, do you want to help us, by helping our customers, and we will pay you for every customer you serve–no fixed hours and just work from home?'

With Gig CX it's possible to do this. You can find the people who love your products and then get them on the team helping your customers.

How does this connect back to the Great Resignation? What is it that people are looking for? They want flexibility and the opportunity to define their own working hours. They want to ditch the commute. They want to be rewarded for what they are doing, rather than just how many hours they sit in a cubicle. They want to work for the brands they love.

All this flexibility is possible in the customer service environment with Gig CX. You don't need to hire people just because they have some customer service experience, then assign them to whichever of your clients needs help first. Turn the model around and hire people who want to work with specific brands. Give them the flexibility to work from home, set their own hours based on how many gigs they want to work on each week and then watch.

You will be creating the Great Attraction–attracting people to come and work for your team because all those agents you onboarded are also advocates and influencers. Think about it. People want flexibility. Give it to them in a way that helps your business and helps the agents.

CHAPTER ELEVEN:

COULD GIG CX BE THE ANSWER TO THE GREAT RESIGNATION?

Fortune magazine recently published a story on the 'great resignation.'[1] This is the period of high employee turnover as workers get more confident about the recovery from the pandemic–alongside more general economic recovery. Young workers are finding the confidence to just quit and find something else.

The data gathered by Fortune is striking. More than half of all Gen Z (18-24) workers want to change their job inside the next year. Only 59% in this age group are satisfied with their job.

A large part of the problem is just the sense of burnout from having to be always-on and always available if their boss sends a text or email, no matter what time it is or how hard they have been focused on their job. Gen Z (57%) and millennials (54%) feel most pressured to be available at all times and are most likely to describe their job as repetitive (65% and 58%, respectively) and tiring (65% for both).

Smaller companies and jobs usually filled with younger people, such as hospitality and contact centers, are struggling to find people at present because of the growing post-pandemic confidence. People don't want to accept inflexible jobs with a boss who expects 24/7 availability. If you are paying minimum wage then forget it.

Entrepreneur magazine recently published advice to small business owners struggling to find people in this labor environment. Their advice was to hire gig workers and the reasons may not be quite what you think.[2] This strategy is all about offering more to the workers, rather than trying to create cost efficiency.

About 36% of US workers are already part of the gig economy, 12% of whom started a freelance job during the Covid pandemic.[3] If growth continues on the same path as now then over half of all American workers will be in independent gig-based work by 2027.

Think about that. If you are running a contact center or a business that has traditionally focused on hiring Gen Z and younger millennials then how can you ignore the prediction that gig workers will soon be in the majority?

Why gig workers and why now? Think for a moment about the great resignation described in Fortune. Why are people leaving their jobs and seeking something better? They are tired of fixed hours, commuting to an office, being judged more on their presence in the office rather than actual performance, seeing that the boss has favorites and some people will never be rewarded. These workers hate the way that office politics has seeped into every aspect of traditional jobs–and how the boss feels they are always on the clock and available.

But people always need a job–unless you are lucky enough to have parents so wealthy that you don't need to work and pay bills.

So what is the gig economy offering? Flexibility, the chance to choose your own working hours so you can work a lot or a little–it's your choice. Being rewarded for what you deliver, not who you know or like. And you don't have a boss calling on Sunday evening, because you set the times you will be available.

Contact centers are directly in the bullseye for the great resignation because they have traditionally offered low wages, high stress, and inflexible hours. Turn that all around and offer people control, flexibility, and the ability to be rewarded for achievements and you can get people on your customer service team that love their job–the complete opposite of the present situation. Earning more and with the flexibility they now demand–what could be better?

CHAPTER TWELVE:

GIG WORKERS ARE CALLING TIME ON THE MONTHLY SALARY CHECK

There is now a pretty strong economic recovery taking place across most industrial sectors, except for those that were really hammered by the pandemic–cruise vacations for example. Companies are gaining confidence.

But this confidence and economic bounce has had another effect. Employees have become footloose. It's possible that this is a direct effect of the pandemic–in the middle of the crisis anyone with a stable job clung on to it. Now that we are seeing a return to some normality, everyone that was thinking about changing job is putting that plan into action.

It's leading to a big problem. Companies are being forced to pay higher rates to attract people and this is leading to faster inflation.[1] More inflation leads to higher wage demands–it can become a vicious cycle if there is no intervention.

But have employee expectations changed? What is it that employees are expecting from their employers now?

We think there are several areas that might explain what some analysts are calling the 'great resignation', but in general it is a dissatisfaction with the inflexibility of a regular job.[2]

The same location, the same hours, the same people. There are some people who thrive on this routine, but many employees now want more.[3] They want to have more flexibility over their hours. They don't want the boss calling them out of hours and they want to be recognized for the work they actually deliver.

This point of recognition is an important one. What happens in a typical salaried job? You know how much you are getting every month. It doesn't matter if you put in a bunch of extra hours and effort to help the team, you are getting the same as always. Plus that pay check only ever arrives once a month on the same day.

Contrast this with the model that gig workers enjoy, especially in an area like Gig CX where LiveXchange is focused. Gig workers are rewarded for the work they actually deliver and they have the flexibility to start or stop whenever they prefer. There is no boss yelling at them because their performance is entirely transparent.

Gig workers earn for each completed gig and gradually add to a balance they can draw from. Rather than waiting for that monthly salary check they can just draw down on the money they have earned at any time. The PayShark system allows LiveXchange to pay people as much or as little as they want to withdraw–directly transferred to their bank account.[4]

So if a gig worker has a busy couple of days and does 20 hours of work they have probably built up a sizable chunk of cash for the completed gigs. They can draw down on their balance and access the funds immediately-in a complete contrast with a typical salaried job.

Some analysts are now suggesting that the entire payments industry is being reshaped by the requirements of gig workers who want smaller, more frequent, payments rather than a fixed amount once a month.[5]

We agree-this is a very important and intelligent insight. The fixed salary model that doesn't reward employees for effort and offers no flexibility around fixed hours feels antiquated when compared to a system that allows you to increase your balance daily and withdraw at any time. If you prefer to just draw on the balance weekly or monthly then that's up to the individual worker, but if you want to get some cash after each couple of days working, that's also no problem.

It's not just the hours and inflexibility that is forcing Gen Z to quit and seek alternative options, it's the inability to access the money owed for work already completed. Gig CX and the broader gig economy will shake up payments and make it possible to facilitate regular transfers as often as people want.

CHAPTER THIRTEEN:

WALMART LAUNCHES NATIONWIDE DELIVERY SERVICE IN THE US

Walmart has announced a plan to commercialize their delivery service.[1] Walmart has spent the past three years refining their national delivery service from over 3,000 stores and now has a system that can quickly reach over 70% of the entire US population.

With this delivery network in place Walmart believes they can offer delivery as a service to other companies–in particular those in more rural areas that have not managed to build an effective network. This would see Walmart directly competing with other delivery services, such as Uber and Doordash.

What we think is really interesting about this is not so much that Walmart wants to take on Uber, but their approach. They are commercializing a network that has been operating deliveries only for Walmart for several years. This is a proven supply chain so corporate customers can feel confident in the Walmart brand and the fact that this service has already been thoroughly tested.

Walmart will also use contract workers, drones, and autonomous vehicles to manage their deliveries. This is really exciting because Walmart has always had an innovative approach when it comes to exploring technology. Their app is one of the most useful in mainstream American retail allowing customers to avoid checkout lines and collect points easily. It could easily be argued that Walmart is the most innovative retailer in the US, except perhaps for Amazon, but then these two companies are quite different.

However, the delivery network is similar to an Amazon idea. Amazon built their own cloud management system as infrastructure for their retail systems before realizing that they could commercialize it as Amazon Web Services (AWS). Now AWS is the biggest cloud Internet company in the world.

Walmart appears to be doing something similar, taking infrastructure they have built and proven for use only by Walmart, and now commercialized it, so other companies will be able to tap into that network.

Walmart will also be using gig workers for deliveries–the company has traditionally resisted embracing the gig economy. It's understandable, because many gig economy companies don't have a great reputation, but we think that it was about time for Walmart to start exploring where some gig workers might be appropriate. The gig economy in 2021 is very different to how it looked before the pandemic.

Almost half of all employed Americans are now working in the gig economy and the wave of recent resignations across the country has demonstrated that many workers really value gig opportunities–they are more flexible than a traditional job with fixed hours.[2] Many more young workers are now interested in choosing their working hours and getting rewarded for each delivery, or each customer served, rather than just picking up the same monthly check.

Walmart has accepted the inevitable. If you want to attract eager employees in 2021 then you need to offer flexibility, recognition, and rewards for doing a great job.

CHAPTER FOURTEEN:

BLACK FRIDAY HOPES AND FEARS ARE HERE AGAIN

Albert Einstein is often credited as once saying: "The definition of insanity is doing the same thing over and over again, but expecting different results."

Whether he actually said it or not doesn't really matter–it's attributed to Einstein because it's exactly the sort of statement he would make. A man with a brilliant mind who identified the failing logic of trying the same solution over and over again and expecting that this time it might work out.

But here we go again. We are just weeks away from Black Friday 2021 and this year should be much bigger than last year because most Covid restrictions have now been lifted. However, take a look at the business journals to see the latest advice on getting customer care teams ready for the holiday season.

Here is a good example[1]–this advice can be summarized as four top tips:

1. Prepare early
2. Support more channels, not just voice calls

3. Hire more people
4. Outsource everything to a contact center specialist

People really publish this as advice? If this is not just doing everything the same old way and hoping for a better result then we don't know how else to describe it. When we published our Gig CX book at the start of this year we included a chapter on this seasonality problem and found pretty much the same type of advice everywhere.[2] Hire more people, cancel overtime, get everyone to work harder. Hope for the best.

As if any of these ideas can really cope with a spike where your customer interactions may increase by several hundred percent just for one or two days. Who is seriously going to expand their contact center from 100 seats to 500 just for a busy weekend?

When Terry featured on the CX Files podcast in June listeners heard the real-life example of New Age in Canada.[3] They had never once managed to cope effectively with Black Friday, no matter how much they asked everyone to pull together. They were making customers wait almost an hour to have calls answered. These are customers calling with their wallet open–imagine how many just give up? Once they deployed Gig CX on top of their core customer service processes–in time for Black Friday 2020–they were answering calls in seconds.

Business journals like Forbes are already warning that the sales and holiday season this year might be a disaster–they are calling it "shipmageddon."[4] Supply chains are making it difficult to obtain enough items to ship on time which means that customer care lines are going to be even busier than usual this year–added to the post-Covid boom.

The US has over 55 million gig workers.[5] The labor is out there. You don't need to make all the same mistakes year after year. You don't need to just shrug and say that Black Friday is always like this–we can never answer all the customer calls.

You simply cannot ignore that the people are out there and available to work on your customer care processes. Don't ignore them and accept that your customer care cannot change.

You don't need to scrap any of your existing customer care processes. If you have an internal team then just augment them with Gig CX when you need extra capacity. Listen to the podcast we mentioned earlier, or check out this summary of the discussion.[6]

If you work with a BPO contact center specialist then you can maintain that relationship–just build extra capacity on top of what they offer by using a gig platform. It's simple and it works.

If your plan for Black Friday 2021 is to follow any of those articles that suggest little more than hoping for the best then good luck–your competitors will be answering the calls you are not taking.

CHAPTER FIFTEEN:

WE NEED A NEW WAY TO THINK ABOUT MEASURING WORK AND PERFORMANCE

Last year the Harvard Business Review published an article about remote working and trust.[1] Many managers were struggling with the sudden move to a work from home (WFH) environment because they either did not trust their team to be doing any work or they did not understand how they could supervise their team without seeing them.

Many companies turned to remote surveillance systems.[2] It sounds very "Big Brother", but many managers only felt comfortable that their team was working if they could observe them using a webcam–usually without the worker knowing when they are being observed and checked on.

Academics have been testing theories around trust and publishing papers as fast as they can.[3] Ignoring the medical catastrophe for one moment, the Covid pandemic has certainly been a bonus for business schools that wanted to test out unusual working conditions.

But what is the thread linking all this research? In every case we are talking abut the need to be seen performing work. All these theories remind me of the production line approach to managing labor and work processes. Managers need to "see" their team. Managers assume that if they can't see their team then they are not working. Team members are judged more favorably based on being present rather than absent.

Everything is focused on presenteeism, being visible, and measuring the amount of time spent on the job.

It reminds me of one of the problems that has plagued the customer service industry for several years now–how do BPOs and CX specialists charge for their services? The traditional measure has always been the Full-Time Equivalent–FTE. This means that if a contact center requires 200 people to operate at a satisfactory level for the client then the client is charged whatever the monthly going rate is for an FTE. This figure will blend together the cost of paying someone their salary along with all the additional operating costs–so the client just sees one figure per person in the contact center.

But what if the BPO reduces the need for people in the contact center by introducing some intelligent automation that handles many simple questions? Or they film some helpful videos answering common questions and load them on YouTube? All these actions can improve the customer experience (CX) and yet they reduce the load on the contact center– so the BPO loses out on FTEs they can charge for if they do the right thing and improve CX.

Almost everyone working in customer service has been grappling with the problems we mentioned earlier–managers struggling to lead their team when they cannot see what the people are doing and even resorting to covert surveillance to ensure they are online and answering calls.

The answer lies in focusing on output rather than time on the job. Designing a customer service solution on the LiveXchange platform is entirely focused on what needs to be delivered for the customer. There is control over hours covered, but this is designed more to match up when agents are needed–so they can pick and choose from times offered. The actual focus is on how many customers are helped and are they satisfied.

You could arrange for one person to be covering a morning shift, another to be covering lunchtime, another in the afternoon, and another in the evening. In a traditional BPO that might be a single FTE, but in this case it could be several people contributing to cover all the required hours.

The companies installing webcams for managers might want to ask why they are still behaving as if everyone is still in the office. Are people still disciplined for arriving online 5 minutes late even if their output is better than colleagues? This focus on time and FTEs doesn't work if your focus is delivering the help that the customer really needs.

CHAPTER SIXTEEN:

IS YOUR CUSTOMER SERVICE OPERATION SUFFERING ANY OF THESE SYMPTOMS?

Brian and Terry have spent a long time thinking about how to explain LiveXchange to the companies that might benefit from their platform. In fact, they even created a list of 'symptoms'–after watching out for potential Covid symptoms this seems like a valid approach.

If you are managing the customer service processes for your organization then do any of these symptoms sound familiar?

- **Seasonal Volume Spikes** (holidays, retail sales, open enrollment, tax season, summer travel etc.) Are there times of the year when your customer service team can't manage even with all hands on deck, more overtime, and vacation bans?
- **Difficult shifts** that nobody wants to work–such as weekends, nights, or holidays.
- **Short volume spikes**–such as a massive increase in volume at lunchtime

- **Below traditional staffing levels**–if you only get one or two enquiries every hour then how do you staff that customer service function? You can't ignore those customers, but can you just pay people to sit waiting?

Any company with any one of these symptoms should certainly explore how Gig CX might be able to help. This applies even more if the training period for your customer service team is relatively short–under two weeks–and you are focusing on areas such as retail, travel, consumer electronics, Healthcare (non-licensed), Technology, eCommerce, or New Economy/Disruptor verticals.

Many companies that Brian and Terry talk to still confuse Gig CX and platforms like LiveXchange as BPO or outsourcing–like you are outsourcing customer service to a contact center company. Let's make it really clear!

1. **You are not outsourcing to an outsourcer.** LiveXchange is a technology marketplace that brings both the "gig" labor and the technology to enable these people to engage with the customer.

2. **LiveXchange is NOT managing these people** YOU are. They are under the same operating model that you use today to manage your direct employees.

3. **You have full visibility and control** over the entire process (Recruiting, Training, Workforce, Operational oversight). We partner you up with people on our staff to assist, but you are in full control.

So if your company faces any of those symptoms then ask yourself, what if we could add a platform on top of our existing processes that allows us to tap into additional customer service resource as and when it is needed. It doesn't replace your existing team or processes–you aren't outsourcing anything. Suddenly those unusual shifts will be easier to fill because you can staff your team using resource across the entire country. You can handle those products when support is infrequent by paying an agent each time they answer a call, rather than for the time waiting for a customer to call. You can build up the team ready to manage the spikes in business, even without changing the team inside your own office.

Seasonal spikes really don't have to be a problem any longer. Are you already planning for Black Friday and the end of year rush?

CHAPTER SEVENTEEN:

JUST ADOPTING WFH IS NOT ENOUGH FOR TRUE FLEXIBILITY

Throughout the most acute period of the Covid pandemic most office-based employees have worked from home (WFH). Many commentators have commented on how successful this experiment was because companies could continue to operate with all their people at home and once they all had Zoom and Teams setup then they could even continue with remote meetings and management.

Once you dig beneath the surface it is clear that the transition to WFH was not completely smooth for every organization. The importance of security was often relegated in the rush to get everyone connected, not every company appreciated the mental health concerns around isolation, and some managers struggled to manage without seeing their team.

It's been quite a learning process for many organizations. Even now that we are seeing a return to offices in many companies, there is a widespread view that companies should adopt more flexibility. This experience proved that home-working is possible so why not allow a mixture of 100% WFH, 100% office, and a hybrid for some employees?

But the thing is, that you don't get true flexibility from WFH alone. Yes, this allows employees to avoid the commute, but are you really going to ask them to sit at a desk at home and just work a straight 8-hour shift as if they had commuted into an office?

This doesn't offer much more flexibility to the workers and it doesn't create any new opportunities for the employer–apart from dropping the commute there is no genuine flexibility.

Imagine if the employer could post a map of all the hours where they need people at the start of each week or month. Everyone on the team can match up what they want to do with the hours being offered by a smart Workforce Management system (WFM).

For example, in a contact center there is usually a quiet period in the afternoon. You get the morning rush, then several quiet hours before the volume of calls picks up again. Traditionally this has to be managed by using an early or late shift, but that also means that a lot of people are underutilized in the afternoon.

What if the contact center manager can reduce how many people are required during the quiet periods and ramp up the offered hours later in the day and early evening? Then the agents can use the WFM system to match up when they want to work, slotting into the available hours.

This means that agents could do 4-5 hours first thing in the morning then take time off in the afternoon–perhaps to fetch the kids from school and make sure they are fed–then add a few more hours afterwards. Split shifts like this are almost impossible to manage when people need to commute, but they really suit a WFH environment.

It's not just the lack of a commute that can make WFH a far more flexible option both for employers and workers. Building greater flexibility into working hours can offer the employer more of a focus on utilizing people when they are needed and offering workers the choice to take hours or entire days off as they prefer.

WFH alone is not the answer.

CHAPTER EIGHTEEN:

BUILDING A GIG MINDSET MEANS CHANGING HOW WE VIEW WORK

Sometimes we wonder if Gig CX is the right name for the kind of flexibility that we see when applying the gig economy to customer service processes. The gig economy is generally seen as a very flexible way to design and manage labor, but most of the time this is seen negatively because risk is pushed from the organization to the individual gig worker.

Uber is a classic example. If it's a quiet night then an Uber driver has no guarantee of any income, so a lot of gig work is seen as precarious and lower value than a traditional Monday to Friday job.

But there is a bigger picture. First, we are sometimes not even comparing apples with apples. Most regular taxi drivers earn more when they are busier-they get more fares and tips so that's only logical. It's not only an effect of the gig economy.

Second, there are many individuals who don't even want a Monday to Friday job. It is the workers themselves that want more flexibility. They are not being exploited, they are matching the hours they want to work to when companies need them. For the customer service roles that the LiveXchange platform manages, companies offer available hours in 30-min chunks and people can select which ones they want to work.

Some people hate the idea of working different hours each week, but there are now many people who want their work to match up to other commitments in their life–they don't want to feel bad about sneaking out of the office at 4pm on Friday because they need to attend an event at their kid's school.

In many ways this demands a kind of mindset change. We need to think less about the hours worked and more about what is actually delivered. In some industries this has been normal for years. Look at journalism. Sure, there are some staffers who just get a monthly salary, but most journalists these days are paid for what they produce, not how many hours they spend sitting at a desk searching for inspiration.

A book published last year really goes into this mindset change in a lot more detail than we can in this chapter. It's called Gig Mindset and is written by Paul Estes.[1] Paul is the Chief Community Officer at Mural, which is a digital workspace for visual collaboration.[2]

Paul's book looks at the gig economy from the perspective of both the companies that are exploring how to work with more gig workers in a way that is positive for both and it also develops the ideas of Tim Ferriss (4-hour work week)–specifically how individuals with specific skills need to present themselves more like small companies, rather than individual employees.[3]

Paul uses a method he calls TIDE in the book. Taskify, Identify, Delegate, and Evolve. This means breaking down your own work and home life into individual tasks that can be defined easily and then using services like Upwork or Fiverr to delegate the tasks to other people.

What Paul is doing here is saying that we may need to revise how jobs work and even how our own life at home is organized. Why spend an hour searching Google for ideas about where to take your kids this weekend when you could pay a few dollars to someone who will create a bespoke top ten list of the best child-friendly attractions nearby?

Mark can remember thinking about this when he and a colleague spent a couple of hours trying to fix a broken printer in the office. There was no IT support available and they needed to print a contract so they were tearing the printer apart trying to figure out the problem. By the time they had fixed it, they realized that between the two of them they had wasted almost an entire day trying to repair the device–it would have saved the company a lot of money if they had just bought a new printer immediately.

This sounds wasteful, but the point is that many of us don't think about the cost of each task because we just get paid the same amount each month anyway. We could spend a day calling clients or fixing a printer–it's all the same. If many more people start adopting the gig mindset then we will see a dramatic shift in the way that work itself is undertaken.

If individuals start expecting their work to be organized around tasks and deliverables then where does that leave the companies still offering a 40-hour week and the same pay each month? Americans are already leaving jobs in their millions because they are not flexible enough–often driven by the flexibility needed for childcare.[4]

The gig mindset could be a large part of the answer. Forget the 8-hour shift and start focusing on what people do–and what they can deliver. Gig CX is already changing how customer service processes can be delivered, but this mindset change needs to go further if the expectations of workers and employers are going to match up in the 2020s.

CHAPTER NINETEEN:

EMPLOYERS AND EMPLOYEES BOTH WANT FLEXIBILITY, SO LET'S BUILD IT!

A few months ago Terry wrote an article titled 'Don't Fear The Gig CX Agent–They Also Love Your Customers!'[1] The message was that Gig CX requires a shift in mindset–it can lead to an improvement in customer service and employee satisfaction, not a decline.

There is always a fear when anyone mentions the gig economy that we are all focused on a race to the bottom. Here we go again with big companies setting the lowest rates and worst possible terms for workers that have no choice...

This is the opposite of the truth. Think about how the world has changed because of the Covid 19 pandemic. Many people have started questioning why they are locked into long hours at the office, contact center, or shopping mall. Commuting time and long shifts just add to the inflexibility of modern working conditions and lead to people that don't really want to be at work just watching the clock all day.

The world has changed. Most people want more flexible hours and more control over their working life, including options like being able to work from home and choosing their hours. Smart employers will sense this change and leverage it. How can employers offer more flexibility so both the worker and company gain from these changes?

Taking a gig approach is a great solution. Throw away the reliance on the clock and this idea that measuring hours at a desk is how you measure productivity. Look around the world at how journalists or graphic designers get paid. They deliver a project and the client pays them. Nobody asks if the work took 30 mins or 8 hours or if they started on it at 9am–there is a value to delivering a piece of work. If the rate isn't worthwhile then they will not take a project with that client again.

If you apply the same kind of model to something like customer service then you can say to the workers–you choose the hours and we will pay you each time you help a customer. Let's forget the need to be at a desk for 8 hours with a bus ride to the office. Stay at home and fit some work around your life.

This approach is exactly what many workers want. They have already decided that they want more flexibility from employers and the old approach wasn't working. Why should it work anyway? We didn't design the long working day for intellectual processes, it came from factories trying to maximize production after the industrial revolution. Isn't it about time we all took a different approach that works for everyone?

The LiveXchange solution is a technology platform that allows companies to build a team of agents and a virtual contact center. You hire the people and you always have complete visibility over them–it's a tool. You set the rates and how many people you need. We are not offering a Business Process Outsourcing (BPO) solution–this is a technology platform that allows you to augment and improve your existing customer service processes.

There are some BPO services out there offering Gig CX. To our mind, that is problematic because it reduces transparency. If you are hiring a service company and you know they are then paying workers for each customer interaction, rather than a time-based salary, then there is a layer between you and the workers that obscures what is going on. If you buy into a platform that lets you control ALL the processes then you know who you are hiring, how much you are rewarding them, and whether they are happy about the arrangement or not.

Getting paid by delivery is a shift in mindset in many industries, including customer service, but it's not problematic if you can ensure that the rates are fair. We know that agents hired this way almost always earn more than they would if paid on a per-hour basis. They get more because they are productive and both the agent and company get the flexibility of not planning work around 8-hour shifts.

Don't be scared of change. Leverage it and build a plan that rewards both your company and the workers who contribute their time and effort. This is not a zero-sum game where one winner forces everyone else to lose.

CHAPTER TWENTY:

A MILLION AMERICANS QUIT THEIR JOB IN JUNE—WHY?

Take a look around at the current labor market. 2020 was the toughest year that many business owners can ever remember, but there is a hiring surge taking place right now as companies across all business sectors see a recovery and scramble to find people.

Ratings agency Fitch has revised numbers[1] upwards for airlines and McDonald's is pushing wages up past $15 an hour and putting pressure on their franchisees to match wages offered in company-owned restaurants.[2] According to the business magazine Forbes recent average wage growth has been strong and almost a million people quit their job in June 2021.[3]

There is a popular view that the labor shortage is because of the unemployment benefits offered during the pandemic, but most economists are suggesting that this is too simplistic. There has been a very strong shift in mindset throughout the pandemic—why else would a million people quit a job they already have to find something else in just the past month? These aren't people at home on the couch watching daytime TV and cashing government checks.

Workers are saying they no longer want to sign non-compete clauses when they are just making sandwiches in a food store, that young serving staff working late evenings should be protected from sexual harassment–they want more flexibility and a better work/life balance. This is not about a generation free-loading on government benefits, the workers have just had enough of jobs that don't pay well and demand inflexible long hours.

Customer service jobs have often fallen into this category. Agent pay has been pretty low because the quiet hours in the day get averaged with the busy periods. But the shifts have generally been inflexible because agents need to commute to a contact center and then work the entire day–busy or not.

The LiveXchange platform addresses all these issues–the need for companies to manage peak customer service periods and the desire from workers for greater flexibility and better rates. How?

Companies with an internal customer service team or contact center know that sometimes it can get crazy. There are peak periods in the day and even peak times of year like the holiday season when it's hard to cope.

With LiveXchange you don't need to replace or change any of your existing internal processes. Keep your agents and contact center, but start considering it as the core of your service team–they are there to serve the "typical" level of customer calls.

Use the platform to augment your physical contact center with a virtual one that seamlessly fits together and allows a team of agents working from home to work alongside your team. You hire and onboard the agents yourself–you are not buying a service from a BPO–you are using a technology platform to improve your existing customer service team. Listen to this recent podcast to hear some real-life views on how easily an existing customer service team can be augmented this way.[4]

This allows your customer service operation to flex as needed. You offer work to the gig agents when you know it will be busy. This means that they can match up the times they want to work with your requirements and so they only work when it will be busy. Getting paid by customer interaction rather than minimum wage means they get the flexibility to choose their hours, work from home, and earn much more than someone commuting daily to a contact center.

Every company leader needs to think about how to manage this labor shortage. You can hike your hourly rates, but that still doesn't give the flexibility and choice over hours that many workers are now looking for.

A system like LiveXchange allows you to retain complete control and visibility over the flexible team so you can transparently augment your existing core team with these extra workers. The core team doesn't get so stressed at peak periods, the gig agents get great work on their terms, and you start answering customer calls immediately.

Take back control of your customer service processes and offer more flexibility to your agents– all at the same time.

CHAPTER TWENTY-ONE:

THE GIG ECONOMY CANNOT BE IGNORED–PEOPLE WANT FLEXIBILITY

Almost half (43%) of American workers are now working in the gig economy according to the International Labor Organization (ILO).[1] The number varies, depending on which research body you choose, but even the more conservative estimates talk about tens of millions of Americans choosing gig work.

But there is a storm brewing because the world is changing quickly. The Labor Secretary Marty Walsh recently said in a Reuters interview: "We are looking at it but in a lot of cases gig workers should be classified as employees... in some cases they are treated respectfully and in some cases they are not and I think it has to be consistent across the board."

Many companies are concerned about working with gig workers because of the recent experience with Uber and Lyft–the United Kingdom decided to force Uber to give drivers the benefits of being employees and the California Proposition 22 created a kind of halfway status–not quite a full employee, but with more benefits that a gig worker.[2]

Most people want to see workers treated fairly. There should never be a race to the bottom in the US. This country has skilled labor that deserves to be respected, but we should also understand that there is an increasing mismatch between what workers want and what employers are delivering.

Terry mentioned in a recent article that almost a million Americans quit their job in June.[3] That's Americans with a job, not people collecting Covid benefits and choosing to not work. There is a hiring frenzy taking place, with employers scrambling to find people, and yet a huge number of people are walking away from their employer.

This is because of a mismatch of expectations. If we define a "good" job as one that offers at least minimum wage and standard benefits then this also comes with an additional set of expectations. The employee needs to commute to a place of work and be there for all the hours the employer expects. They can't leave early on Wednesday to collect their kids from school or attend a children's event on Friday.

This inflexibility in regular jobs is one of the major reasons why the gig economy has grown so large. If the ILO estimate is correct, almost half of all American workers cannot be ignored. We can't assume they all want 8-hour-shifts for five days a week. There is a reason why people are looking for work that fits their lifestyle.

The answer is not as simple as just suggesting that all these gig workers are offered full-time employment contracts. In most cases this is not what they want. They want complete flexibility to define when and where they work and they are happy to be rewarded based on what they deliver, not necessarily how much time they spend on the job.

It's a different way of thinking about work, but it's certainly not abusing the worker if rates are fair. The problem with the gig economy comes from services like restaurant delivery services paying extremely low rates to workers expected to rush around on a bike making deliveries all day. We all know what bad gig work looks like.

Clearly there are examples like this where protection may be required, but the protection may not need to be full employment status–it could be a protected legal minimum value for each gig.

This different way of thinking is really stark with the Gig CX approach that our LiveXchange platform facilitates. Think about the normal way that companies find agents to work in a contact center–they hire for general intelligence, friendliness, and ability to speak clearly. They train the agent in the product that needs to be supported after they have found and hired all those friendly-sounding people.

Our approach is more like the reverse. If you run a fashion brand then we can find people who love fashion–even those who love your brand in particular. They already know about the products. They just need training on the system and processes involved in customer interactions. They can also be based anywhere, not just within commuting distance of a contact center.

It's an entirely different approach to work. These people are interested in the brands they are working with, they are choosing their hours, and they can work from home. Their rates are far higher than anyone working in a traditional contact center and being rewarded for each hours sitting at a desk.

The legal debate about gig workers will continue, but it's a shame to see this as an employer vs employee argument. Worker rights can be respected and workers can get the flexibility they now want. If employer and employee both want flexibility and to move away from the Monday to Friday fixed hours approach to employment then we need to think about what this means for everyone–not just assume that employers are trying to exploit people.

The agents working on the LiveXchange platform are far more satisfied than the average agent based in a contact center. They earn more, they work from home, they set their own hours, they can select the brands they work with. They are not asking the Labor Secretary to make them employees.

Let's start thinking about how work needs to be structured so it offers the flexibility that post-pandemic employees want and also ensures that they are respected and rewarded fairly. Our platform is a great start.

CHAPTER TWENTY-TWO:

WFH SECURITY REQUIRES MORE THAN JUST FIREWALLS

Before 2020, many companies executives were very concerned about encouraging work-from-home (WFH) because of the security implications. Most companies built a strong firewall around their corporate network and all the connections into individual homes were seen as potential ways in through the firewall.

The pandemic has proven that distributed security is possible. Just about every office-based employee had to work from home, so network security managers quickly devised a more sophisticated approach to securing communications.

But what about contact centers?

If you have a physical contact center inside your office then the argument goes that you can monitor the workers and secure all the network traffic. Hiring agents that work from home just opens just creates an insecure environment, doesn't it?

This doesn't have to be true. Take a look around the world at how all the BPOs operated over the past year–and continue to do so. If you hired any one of the major contact center specialists to manage your customer service processes then you have watched them move all the agents into their homes during the pandemic.

The BPOs managed. We haven't heard about any major data leak caused by contact center agents being moved into their home during the pandemic. It is possible and there are three key areas you need to think about if you want confidence of security:

- **People:** any agents that join our platform are checked and vetted. We don't just check their employment history, we ensure their background checks out and there is no history of criminal activity. We know that anyone connecting to the network is exactly who they say they are.
- **Network:** a distributed approach to security has to be applied, rather than relying on the office firewall. This means ensuring that the agent connecting can only use the LiveXchange system–effectively shielding the entire operating system from anything else on the device. Nothing can be copied, downloaded, or printed locally.
- **Process:** applying industry standard security protocols is the key to ensuring that customer information is secure every time. Our processes match the required PCI Level 1 compliance–the highest level of protection for processing payment cards and we are constantly exploring new ways to improve beyond these requirements.[1]

Creating a secure WFH environment is about much more than just network security alone. In fact, even the traditional contact center environment should be as robust as this, although we know this is not always the case. There is an assumption that the network firewall offers a large degree of protection in the office environment, but without the strongest protocols and checks on who is working inside the office the security of your customer data can be compromised.

The past year has proven that WFH can be secure if it is well planned. We are happy to explain to anyone exactly how many procedures we follow to ensure that everyone working on the LiveXchange platform is secure.

CHAPTER TWENTY-THREE:

THE GLOBAL TALENT CRUNCH MEANS THAT JOBS NEED TO BE REDEFINED

It's been clear for a number of years that there is a war for highly skilled talent, but this has been exacerbated by the Covid-19 pandemic. Some skilled workers are changing career, some are demanding greater flexibility about where they work, and some are giving up on the idea of a job needing to be a regular Monday to Friday commitment.

This is affecting companies of all sizes. Look at how the Swiss bank UBS just announced the permanent adoption of hybrid and flexible working hours and locations (office or home or WeWork) for most of their employees.[1] What is interesting is that the UBS management are explicit about why they are doing this–they believe that they can attract talent away from the more rigid Wall St banks that are mostly heading back into their offices and suits.

Korn Ferry just published a research paper suggesting that if you look at all the major economies globally then by the end of this decade there will be more than 85 million skilled jobs vacant–companies unable to find people to perform these roles.[2] The cost to businesses of not getting productive people into these roles could be worth more than the combined GDP of Japan and Germany.

Korn Ferry highlights the USA as having a deficit already–up to around 6m positions unfilled–but this is likely to double by the end of the decade. Countries such as Brazil and Indonesia are predicted to be in an even worse situation with many more vacancies than people available with the right skills.

You can follow the link in the references to read the entire Korn Ferry report (titled 'The Global Talent Crunch') for yourself, but it's worth quoting a short part of the conclusion: "We will see successful organizations moving from a paternalistic approach to a more mature, flexible relationship with their people, built on mutual respect. We can also expect a more fluid labor market, with staff brought in on a per-project basis. For individuals to remain credible, it will be critical for them to stay constantly up to date, with the emphasis on individual responsibility for maintaining relevant skills."

We think the conclusion from this research is heading down the right path. There is a global talent crunch and we will never solve it just by creating more job vacancies. A fully joined up approach from education into employment is required, but this also needs employers to think carefully about how the employer-employee relationship works in the 2020s.

A job isn't something the employee should be doing for the same number of hours in the same place each day, always feeling grateful that their pay check arrives on time each month. Skilled employees have options and employers need to recognize this and reflect their appreciation for the fact that people want to work for them–look at the concrete steps a bank like UBS is taking just so they can say at every job interview 'working with us isn't like being with one of those Wall St companies.'

These options are increasingly global. Graphic designers no longer just design art campaigns for clients in their home city–the market for skilled people is truly global and this not only creates some amazing opportunities to accelerate development, it also means that skilled people have a potentially global pool of clients.

LiveXchange has worked on this basis for a long time. We don't search for people who live near to a specific office. The people can stay at home and set the hours they want to work. When we want to find some really specific skills to support a client, it's no problem because we can search globally.

What if you want to build a customer service team that has really intimate knowledge of gaming and Augmented Reality? We can find fans of Pokémon GO and onboard them and let them contribute when they want to. Try finding this kind of expertise if you are limited to everyone within a few miles of your office.

The Korn Ferry research is just illustrating the problem. If companies don't change then they will no longer be able to find the people they used to take for granted. The global talent crunch is real and it needs a new approach to building teams that can deliver for modern companies.

CHAPTER TWENTY-FOUR:

TACKLING SEASONALITY HEAD-ON WITH GIGCX

A recent episode of the CX Files podcast described how a major Canadian e-commerce brand, NewAge Products, faced a problem that is familiar to many companies.[1] Their contact center was scaled to be the right size for most of the year, but their business has two peak seasons.

NewAge is focused on garage and garden furniture–all those cupboards, shelves, and general organization you need at home. They ramp up when people are interested in the sales–meaning from Black Friday through to the early part of the New Year–and then also around the spring and early summer. That's when people are thinking, 'I'm going to get the garden organized so we can have a great summer outside.'

The problem is that if a contact center is designed to handle the average call volume then you can end up with all these opportunities to drive revenue being missed. Who wants to wait on the phone for an hour when you are trying to give a brand your cash? It's too easy for customers placed on hold to find an alternative or to just give up and not bother ordering.

As Mahesh Raghuram, Director of Customer Service, NewAge Products explained on the podcast it took them just two or three weeks to overlay a Gig CX layer on top of their existing contact center processes.[2] This meant that they could keep all their existing processes, for all the regular times of the year, but every time they expect interest to ramp up, the Gig CX layer can be activated.

The bottom line is that customers during the last Black Friday sales period in November 2020 were being answered in seconds.

We have often talked about seasonality in this and our previous book, but we think there are still some customer service managers that think they can throw everything at the problem and get past it. Typical advice is increased overtime, no vacations allowed at key periods, every possible team member on the calls–including some temporary hires if you can squeeze them into the contact center.

None of this works if your peak period sees demand increasing by multiples of the average. If your Black Friday sales are 350% of your normal sales then you cannot realistically scale up your service team to cope just by asking everyone to do some overtime.

As the NewAge example shows really clearly, you can fix the problem without needing a major transformation of your existing processes. If they work well for 9 months of the year then that's fine– no need to change. Just build a pool of talent that you can call on for those peak periods and you can ensure that the customer experience remains great for all 12 months of the year.

CHAPTER TWENTY-FIVE:

#GIGCX: LIVEXCHANGE FEATURED ON THE CX FILES PODCAST

Terry recently participated in a really interesting episode of the CX Files podcast focused on the present and future of Gig CX.[1] It featured Terry alongside Mahesh Raghuram[2], Director of Customer Service, NewAge Products and Vinay Gupta[3], Senior Expert, McKinsey & Company. As the host, Mark Hillary[4] introduced the session he made a note to point out that the three guests represent one of the leading advisory companies in the world, a leading Gig CX platform, and a leading e-commerce brand that actually uses Gig CX–what a great combination on one show!

Vinay introduced the podcast by defining Gig CX, but if you have seen our earlier book then you already know what it is.[5] It really got moving when Mahesh explained why he had explored Gig CX in the first place. He said: "One thing we wanted to introduce to our customer service model was flexibility. We are an e-commerce company with a high average order value, which means we have massive seasonal peaks. If you look at a Black Friday timeframe or the start of summer, then we would struggle. Customers will probably wait for 30 to 60 minutes, on average. So we needed more flexibility without getting tied into the FTE requirements of traditional BPO."

Mahesh also noted that the time required for an agent to be fully operational is usually about 90-120 days, but the Gig CX agents are usually fully productive inside 28-42 days. That in itself is impressive because you can already see that it only takes a third of the time to onboard new people.

Vinay explained that Gig CX offers an opportunity both to in-house contact center managers and also BPOs. The commonly-held idea that Gig CX is a replacement for everything else is wrong. He said: "From a BPO point of view, given this market is going to be very mature very soon, they need to ramp up their capability. If I'm a BPO andI don't have a flexible workforce, clients might just go to another BPO. It's important for BPOs to invest in this capability and bring it up to a level where they can offer start offering it to their clients."

All these points from Vinay are really important. Gig CX is maturing and becoming trusted. It's also becoming clear that this is not an either or decision. You can keep your internal contact center or work with a BPO–either way, the solution can become more flexible if it is augmented with Gig CX.

Mahesh actually described the process of augmenting his own contact center. He said: "It was fairly simple. It just layered in perfectly on top of our existing contact center model. And we were able to get it up and running in about two to three weeks." He added: "We've actually reported well over satisfactory service levels throughout the peak season, so we were answering calls in under 45 seconds, from November, all the way till the end of January."

We think these are the two key points to make in this chapter:

1. You can move from a situation where customers are waiting an hour to be served to answering them in seconds.

2. You don't need to change your existing customer service model—just layer the Gig CX solution over the top and use that as your flexibility buffer.

Search for CX Files on your favorite podcast app to replay the entire episode for yourself—scroll back to June 2021 to find the episode.

CHAPTER TWENTY-SIX:

WFH ALLIANCE DELIVERS A STRONG BOOST TO WFH CULTURE

Terry saw a great webinar recently that was hosted by the WFH Alliance.[1] It was titled 'WFH 2.0: From Staffing Strategy To Workplace Strategy.' The event featured some examples, including Marriott Hotels, of companies that usually started exploring a Work-From-Home (WFH) solution as a way to find more staff, but then they found that it created a positive cultural shift in the entire company.

Throughout the pandemic, there have been a lot of stories about people that have not enjoyed the WFH experience. Younger employees that still live with their parents, or live in shared accommodation, have generally been keen to get back to some office space, rather than working in a bedroom.

But as the WFH Alliance described, once we start moving on from the emergency response and actually start hiring people to work from home then a big change emerges. These people want to be at home. They are prepared to create the right space for home working. They appreciate the flexibility of being judged far more for what they deliver, rather than how many hours they spend on the job.

The latest Harvard Business Review podcast did a deep dive on some of the challenges and advantages of WFH and this idea of a cultural shift in how people are managed was one of the most fundamental.[2] In fact, Nicholas Bloom, a professor from Stanford University, said that managing people by supervising their hours and time contributed–watching them arrive at 9am for an 8-hour shift and penalizing the late starters–is impossible in a WFH environment.

Some companies have attempted it, but it involves managers using cams to watch over their team. It really sounds like a modern Big Brother and has no place in a team that wants to build a great working culture of trust and transparency.

But the real point that Terry took away from the webinar was that if you hire people who want to work from home and value the flexibility this allows them then you will not have any of the common problems we saw mentioned throughout the pandemic–isolation and burnout and attempts to recreate the office environment from home.

Building WFH into your corporate strategy is no longer just a simple staffing solution that allows to you find talent anywhere–although this remains a good reason to use it. WFH builds a more transparent management culture and can improve communication between teams. Many detractors of WFH argue that the 'water cooler moments' are where the real innovation happens, but how often have you ever really seen innovation in your company because of a water cooler conversation?

The trust and respect that is needed to make WFH work leads to more idea sharing and team discussion–that's where your innovation and new ideas can really come from.

Building a WFH strategy isn't just about hiring more people than you can locate in your office, it's about changing the way your company does business and making it more engaging and flexible for everyone. WFH is one of the foundations of a modern GigCX strategy–this is how the modern workplace can be designed and improved.

CHAPTER TWENTY-SEVEN:

INDUSTRY DISRUPTORS NEED DISRUPTIVE IDEAS TO MANAGE CX

CNBC just announced their 2021 Disruptor 50 list.[1] These are the companies with business models and growth rates that are aligned with the rapid pace of modern technological change. In short, these companies are disrupting the industries they operate within by embracing emerging technology and rewriting the conventional rules of business.

Robinhood comes in first.[2] It's no surprise because Robinhood has barely been out of the headlines in recent months. When Reddit traders started buying GameStop shares in huge numbers Robinhood became known as the app that makes it easy for anyone to trade on the markets.[3]

Stripe takes second place.[4] Often called the GDP of the Internet, Stripe built a developer-focused instant payment platform that makes it easy for online services to process payments. You have probably used Stripe and are not even aware of it. If you have used Amazon, Slack, or Shopify then you certainly have.

We always think about services like this and wonder why the incumbent players didn't do anything. Did the banks really think that their decades-old payment system was going to work for e-commerce? Why didn't they do something?

It's like the Kodak story from almost a decade ago. Kodak invented the digital camera, but when they finally launched digital photography services it wasn't to encourage online sharing, it was to offer customers a printed version of an online photo.[5] When Kodak filed for bankruptcy in 2012, Facebook was in the process of acquiring Instagram for $1 billion.

As you go down the Disruptor 50 list there are some familiar and some less familiar names. Patreon is helping creators earn online. NuBank is reimagining banking in Latin America. Impossible Foods is creating meat without the need for animals. Discord is using audio to connect people.

One thing connects all these brands. They are growing fast and they are reshaping their own industry, but how are they building a customer service function that can scale with that hyper-growth?

Look around at some other disruptors like Spotify, Casper, Peloton, Airbnb, or Birchbox. They all need to offer fantastic service to their customers, in fact we would argue that these highly visible and disruptive brands need to go above the customer service standards you might expect from your local bank. It's in their DNA.

Building a customer service function with a BPO isn't going to be easy for any of these brands. They want strong control over their own customer experience because they are shaping the future of their industry–these are not normal brands. They want a strong ability to recruit digitally so the hiring process can scale quickly. They also need flexibility. If you sign a deal to manage 400 agents in a Las Vegas contact center then what happens when the client turns around and says 'hey we went into 80 new markets overnight...' Spotify did that in February. Imagine adding multilingual customer support for 80 new markets overnight.[6]

Gig CX is the only way to go for disruptive brands.[7] The CX process can remain in-house and close to the brand. The agents can be distributed nationally or internationally, allowing multilingual options and new market support. The recruitment process is entirely digital and can scale to any size. If you want to enter new markets then you can just onboard some new agents in those locations without any requirement to sign new BPO contracts.

Disruptors need disruptive CX.

CHAPTER TWENTY-EIGHT:

BUILDING A GIG CX ADVOCACY NETWORK ENHANCES BOTH CX AND DIVERSITY

We have often written in the past[1] about Gig CX not being a replacement for Business Process Outsourcing (BPO) and contact centers. These ideas can co-exist and in many cases we are working with BPOs to create solutions where they build out the heart of a customer service solution and we add the flexibility–this works really well.

But there is a lingering idea in the marketplace that Gig CX is a replacement for an internal contact center or just competes with an outsourced contact center. I'd like to suggest a new idea. There are some areas in the customer journey where Gig CX can complement a traditional customer service strategy and there are many people who love working in a Gig CX environment–they would never work in a contact center.

Think about a classic customer journey:

- **Awareness:** the customer first learns about your product
- **Research:** the customer reaches out for more information, either directly to the brand or from social networks and online searches
- **Purchase:** the customer buys it
- **Support:** the customer needs help with a problem or has a question

That's the traditional linear customer journey and in the modern world this is now much more jumbled and circular. Customers are not only searching, comparing, and reading social media and reviews, but also creating all this content too.

But this also means that your customer engagement is now far more often at many different points in the customer journey–not just post-purchase support calls to a contact center. How do you meaningfully engage with a customer that has not purchased anything, but just wants to ask a few questions? Or a loyal customer that keeps getting in touch just because they love engaging with your brand? How do these interactions even fit into your traditional contact center metrics anyway?

What about if you are selling big ticket items? A car, a visit to a luxury resort, a wedding venue, or a property? Imagine the power of introducing a potential customer with questions to an existing or previous customer. You want information on a car and the car manufacturer says 'here, talk to Dave, he owns that model...' Or you are thinking of booking an expensive conference suite at a hotel because you are organizing a wedding and the venue introduces you to a customer that used the venue last year.

Think about the level of advocacy this creates. You are offering an impressive level of service to the potential customer, but also involving that advocate network in helping to promote your brand. You can pay them a fixed fee every time they help out or pay them in reward points or create some other form or recognition. It's up to you, but the actual connectivity can be organized using a platform like LiveXchange.

Imagine how this can improve your engagement throughout the entire customer journey and it complements your existing customer service strategy–you don't need to replace anything.

You can get some great people on your bench, all batting for your products. People who love your brand and would never think of working 40-hours a week in a contact center. You can find fans on Instagram and ask if they want to help out a few times a week, real experts that know your products inside out. You can tap into the enormous pool of retired citizens with deep knowledge but no desire to spend all day working.

This also offers an opportunity to genuinely embrace diversity and inclusion. We all know that companies talk about diversity on their website, but how many are actively doing something meaningful? If you augment your customer service operation with a Gig CX team then you can hire people far from your neighborhood office. You can hire people that face a physical challenge commuting twice a day, you can use the expertise of people who struggle with non-visible illness by allowing them to contribute without needing to commit to a full day.

Gig CX can augment your existing CX strategy to build an advocacy program that rewards loyal customers and delights potential customers alike.

CHAPTER TWENTY-NINE:

IRS CUSTOMER SERVICE IS SO BAD FORBES CALLED IT 'DIRE' IN A HEADLINE

The May 17th IRS deadline has now passed. Hopefully you managed to get your taxes filed on time this year. If you did then it is probably thanks to one of the various software systems that makes it easier, rather than the IRS customer service and helpline team.

Forbes magazine recently profiled customer service at the IRS and actually called it 'dire' in their headline.[1] Here are some of the statistics the Forbes profile focuses on:

- 7 in 100 calls are being answered on their toll-free account management helpline
- 2% of calls are being answered on the 1040 helpline (individual tax returns)
- A 20-minute minimum wait time on hold if you are one of the lucky 2% to get through
- 300% increase in calls to the helpline this filing season
- 21 days to process electronic returns–don't hold your breath for that refund

We don't think that we have ever heard of such awful customer service performance metrics. We have all called customer service and cursed as we are forced to wait a few minutes for service, but these numbers are incredible. Only one in fifty callers is actually getting through to the IRS helpline?

Imagine if Amazon only bothered processing your basket one in fifty times and just ignored you every other time you clicked the purchase button? At least with a private company you normally have a choice to purchase goods or services elsewhere. With the IRS, nobody has any choice other than calling fifty times to get through.

Only the federal government could offer a service like this to citizens and get away with it. US citizens really deserve better than this. They deserve respect.

There is another way and it doesn't require outsourcing. It's also fast to setup and extremely flexible. It can be reduced during the quiet period of the year when there are few calls and ramped up for filing season. It's Gig CX.[2]

There are so many qualified accountants and tax experts out there that could be quickly trained in IRS procedures. Imagine creating a bench of hundreds, or even thousands, of these experts and then putting the systems and security in place so they can help citizens from their own home.

The IRS can retain control over the agents and use a virtual contact center in the cloud to match citizen callers to agents. It's easy to setup and doesn't require real estate for contact centers or lengthy negotiations with contractors.

The IRS needs new ideas. Filing season 2022 doesn't need to be like this. They need a flexible solution that they can retain control over and they need the processes and security that ensures citizen data is safe. They need a solution like the LiveXchange platform.

They need Gig CX.

CHAPTER THIRTY:

GIG CX IS DIFFERENT TO THE GIG ECONOMY LAWMAKERS UNDERSTAND

The industry analyst Gartner has predicted that by 2025 gig workers will make up around 40% of the entire US workforce.[1] This sounds scary if your idea of a career is a linear progression from junior to more senior roles and a corner office that helps you coast to retirement.

But millennials and Generation Z are now the majority of the workforce in the US.[2] They want opportunities and fulfilling work, but they don't necessarily want it to involve a long commute and ten-hour days in an office. The Covid-19 pandemic has showed more traditional organizations that they can embrace more flexibility and still remain productive. Working patterns are changing.

Before the pandemic, the freelancing platform Upwork explored attitudes to work in the US and they found that 76% of their freelancers are much happier with freelance work, rather than a regular job working 40-hours a week for the same employer.[3] A common criticism is that these people are only freelancing because they can't find a regular job, but the Upwork data shows that the majority of freelance knowledge workers say they are satisfied with the amount of work they're bringing in and are optimistic about the future of independent work.

- 72% have the amount (or more) of work that they want
- 92% expect work opportunities for freelancers to increase in the future
- 90% believe the best days are ahead for freelancing

We believe that this support for more flexible work will only have been increased by the pandemic-we can see this in the frequent statements from major companies allowing their employees to now work from home.[4] But the conventional view from traditional labor commentators and legislators is that flexible labor is detrimental, or even abusive, for the workers. Many see the gig economy as dangerous and try to introduce new controls-an example is AB5 and how it affects ride sharing in California.[5]

We are not suggesting that we don't need any legislation to protect workers. Workers do need protection, but there is also a need to explore why so many younger workers actively want more flexible jobs-we can't just ignore this. They really don't want to be trudging into the same office day after day. If these people are seeking greater flexibility, how do we design legislation that protects the new reality of work rather than trying to force Uber drivers to become employees of Uber.

The gig economy is often seen as a race to the bottom. Algorithms are handing out jobs to humans who get paid as little as possible. Unfortunately, in some areas of the gig economy this stereotype is close to the truth. We don't think any of those delivery drivers handing you a Chinese takeaway on a Friday night are swimming in cash or feeling that they have much agency over their working life.

But this is the problem–our general perception. When we see that more people prefer freelance and flexible work many legislators, politicians, and even managers, immediately think of the restaurant delivery guy out in the rain delivering takeaways.

The gig economy is broader and deeper than this. Look at my area–Gig CX. Gig CX has become the standard term for platform-focused customer service using virtual contact centers. Maybe the name needs to change because what we are doing is far from the gig economy that causes concern.

We hire smart people to support brands. They are often fans of the companies they are supporting. They are educated and able to pick and choose which brands they want to work with and for how many hours each week. It's entirely flexible. When a company builds a bench of experts to support their products they don't just offer minimum wage to these people. Our people, working on the basis where they get paid each time they help a customer, earn far more than the equivalent customer service agent in a contact center on a regular salary.

Let's repeat that. Gig CX agents earn more than salaried customer service agents. This is no race to the bottom. The agents prefer this flexibility and they earn more. This is a war for the best talent and this talent is well-rewarded for their service.

Legislators that still frown every time someone mentions the gig economy should explore Gig CX and realize that people want the flexibility that a gig platform offers. They would never go to work everyday in an office.

These are great jobs–just ask our people!

CHAPTER THIRTY-ONE:

THE TSA IS PREPARING FOR A SUMMER BOOM IN TRAVEL–IS YOUR CX READY?

Have you seen just how many new officers the US Transportation Security Administration (TSA) is hiring? They are currently trying to hire over 6,000 new officers and it looks like they will not be able to hit these recruitment targets before the summer travel boom.[1]

The TSA would screen about 2.5 passengers a day before the pandemic, but they are already screening around 1.5m a day right now. Americans are starting to travel again and the forecasts that predicted a recovery over several years are already looking pessimistic.

What does this mean for the travel industry and airlines?

A great summer, hopefully. However, while it's great to see people traveling again and booking flights, the rapid recovery may be taking some of these companies by surprise. Many airlines laid off pilots, cabin crew, and customer service specialists because there were no passengers in the middle of the pandemic. How are they going to ramp up faster than expected?

We can't help with the pilot situation–over half of all commercial pilots were grounded by the pandemic and many lost their jobs.[2] Many ended up in jobs with no relation to aviation–like picking onions or stacking supermarket shelves.[3] Although with so many unemployed pilots around the world now, we guess it should be fairly easy to entice them back into flying again. Picking onions sounds like tough work.

However, there is an extremely rapid way to ramp up the customer service function for the airlines. Use a Gig CX strategy to quickly onboard and train agents who work from their own home using their own devices.

In the time it would take to Covid-proof a new contact center you could have already hired and trained everyone you need to cope with the wave of travel that the TSA hiring spree is forecasting.

A Gig CX approach will allow you to just focus on finding the right people and training them, not worrying about which customer service partner you should choose or where to locate a contact center. You can hire anyone from anywhere, allowing you to raise the bar and choose from the best. By offering much more flexible working hours and the ability to work from home you will also insure against future attrition–people with more flexibility in their working life tend to be much more satisfied with their job.

The TSA recruitment boom shows that almost everyone thinks this summer will be busy for the travel industry, but if you want to respond to this demand quickly and then build more flexibility into your customer service then you can't just return to the old strategies that worked in 2019.

CHAPTER THIRTY-TWO:

TITLE: GIG CX CAN HELP YOU ENGAGE EARLIER WITH CUSTOMERS

The rules controlling the US and Canada border have been dramatically increased since the outbreak of the Covid-19 pandemic. The various quarantine and stay at home measures used to control the spread of the virus mean that the border was entirely closed to all but the most essential visitors.

Talks are ongoing to figure out how to safely reopen the border, but news from the discussions indicates that it may not happen quickly.[1] Without a clear strategy it seems the default will be to continue blocking all non-essential travel.

There are over 100 legal border crossings between Canada and the US and daily border crossings are down by over 80% now, compared to pre-pandemic.[2] The rules that define who can travel include exceptions such as essential business, family reunions, and funerals, but they are fairly complex.[3] This has created a situation where people often need to ask the government for advice before traveling.

This is an interesting and quite different approach to citizen (or customer) service. We often see organizations focused on the customer interaction being after a transaction has taken place, like a customer calling for help after a purchase, but in some cases the individual citizen or customer needs advice BEFORE traveling or making a purchase.

The wait times for advice right now are horrific. We have read about people waiting for hours just to determine if they are allowed to cross the border or not. The problem is that if the rules are not extremely simple and clear then there is a need to ensure that advice can be easily obtained. In this case, it's clearly failing.

This is a really good example of a situation where a Gig CX solution could work. Agents can receive their training in the rules determining who can travel and who cannot. They can then be brought on stream using a safe, virtual, contact center so there is no need to build out a traditional contact center. The amount of personal data being managed is extremely minimal so security is not a primary concern for this type of advisory service.

We also know that the need for this service will eventually decline, although nobody knows how long it will be required. With all these uncertainties and the present overloaded advisory system it looks more and more like a Gig CX solution would be the fastest way to scale up support from more agents, and to ramp up or down as required.

Outside of government, we believe that many consumer brands need to think more about this pre-purchase contact and support. Think in more detail about the customer journey–how are customers learning about your products and how do they get advice or information before making a purchase?

Why not recruit some Gig CX agents that you know are already fans of your brand–maybe some micro-influencers? Offer them the chance to educate potential customers who have questions and you can quickly start building a strong network of advocacy. It's low risk because you only need to pay agents when they help a customer, but think of the powerful opportunity you will have to shape the customer opinion of your brand–someone calls for advice and connects to a real expert. That's a powerful signal to send before a purchase.

As the US and Canada border control issues demonstrate, sometimes people just need good advice and that advice can really influence their decision. If you want to interact with customers long before a transaction takes place then Gig CX is a good way to build that support.

CHAPTER THIRTY-THREE:

BPOS SERVING AGILE CUSTOMERS IN THE DIGITAL ECONOMY NEED THE FLEXIBILITY OF GIG CX

E-commerce is booming all across the world. This rapid growth was accelerated by the Covid-19 pandemic–as traditional in-store retail became more difficult because of the pandemic restrictions, shopping online suddenly became more attractive. Some analysts have suggested that the growth in e-commerce in the past year was what they had earlier predicted for the next five years.

According to the U.S. Commerce Department, sales in online retail in 2020 grew by 44% on 2019, hitting a value of US$861 billion last year compared to US$598 billion the year before. Meanwhile, Canada registered a hike of 72.7% in online spending – excluding foodservice and catering purchases – making it the fastest growing e-commerce market on the planet.

It's more than just a boom–this is an extremely rapid acceptance that the digital economy is now an essential part of consumer lifestyles. These companies and consumer behaviors are here to stay.

This article in Nearshore Americas details how the Business Process Outsourcing (BPO) industry has responded to the boom.[1] In many cases it looks like BPOs are focusing their attention on digital economy and e-commerce clients because this area is growing so fast. As this sector grows, all these companies need to build a more robust customer service function and the BPOs are the natural partner for this.

But nobody can deny that the BPOs were caught out in 2020. Many of them took months to adapt to the new working environment, especially the need to support agents working from home.

We believe that if the BPOs want to avoid future difficulties then they need to explore a Gig CX strategy, even if it supports a more traditional contact center at the core. There are several reasons why we believe the BPOs can drastically improve the service offered to their clients if they blend Gig CX into their service:

- **Flexibility:** you can ramp up and ramp down without any problems–the gig agents are paid as they help customers and they work from home, so you don't need to worry about expanding the size of the contact center or paying extra people to work extra 8-hour shifts.
- **Resilience:** spreading the customer service function across a distributed team has obvious advantages–this approach would have prevented the problems many BPOs faced in 2020.

- **Attrition:** when you hire people who like the products they are supporting, want to work from home, and have greater control over their working hours, you get people who are committed and want to stay on the team.
- **Expertise:** you can hire from anywhere so you can choose the best and can also seek out people who already love the products they will be supporting.
- **Advocacy:** hiring fans of the brand has another advantage–it allows you to build out a community of people who actively love the brand and tell friends about it.

Gig CX is not an either/or decision. You don't need to choose Gig CX or choose a BPO, but we believe BPOs that blend some Gig CX into their service can offer a dramatically more agile service than those relying on a traditional contact center alone. Given that we are talking about clients in the digital economy that are managing extremely fast growth this could be a significant benefit for the BPOs and their clients.

CHAPTER THIRTY-FOUR:

TITLE: HOW DO YOU BUILD A FLEXIBLE CONTACT CENTER IF YOU DON'T WANT TO USE OUTSOURCING?

Business journals and consulting firms are always advising companies to use outsourcing as a business strategy. This orthodox approach to corporate strategy has been around for decades, but was really codified in 1994 when Gary Hamel and CK Prahalad published 'Competing for the Future.'[1]

This book, from Harvard Business School Press, gave us the theory of 'core competence' which basically means that if someone else can manage your payroll or IT better than you can do it yourself then pay them to do it. This frees up your time and resource to focus on what you can do better than others–your core competence.

A recent example is this feature in Forbes.[2] The article offers five tips on how to more effectively outsource your business processes. They are pretty simple guidelines such as making sure the management want to do this and defining your goals before starting the project, but the point is that these tips are now just a part of the conventional wisdom–very few managers ever question this guidance.

But what if you are managing your business processes around customer service? What if you don't want to outsource to a partner company for a number of reasons? Maybe you want to keep a tight control on quality, or maintain your corporate culture when talking to the customer, or just ensure that the interface between the customer and your brand remains internal?

Contact centers don't automatically need to be outsourced. If you are managing your customer service processes internally and then seeing articles like this in Forbes and wondering if your strategy is correct then there are other options.

Gig CX allows you to retain control internally, but with the flexibility to manage costs and maximize efficiency.[3] You can scale up and down as needed, so a flexible e-commerce company that has always struggled with Black Friday no longer needs to worry. The answer doesn't have to be outsourcing to an enormous contact center specialist, retain your team in-house and work with a Gig CX model.

The LiveXchange platform is a great example of what is possible.[4] You can use the platform to onboard and train new agents and alert your pool of agents to shifts that are available–controlling the shifts down to each 30 minutes. Your agents are working from home and because you can control the recruitment process you can ensure that they support and engage with your style of corporate culture.

If your industry, or even your own company, has fans or social media influencers then you can even approach these people–ask the influencers if they want to help customers of the brand they already love. They don't need to do 40-hours a week in a contact center, they can just do a few hours a week if that's all they want to contribute–it's entirely flexible. They can become brand ambassadors.

The point is that you can use the platform to build a virtual contact center that brings your existing agents together with a pool of Gig CX agents that flex up and down as needed. They are your recruits and you manage them all. There is no outsourcing required and yet you can still build more flexibility into your customer service processes.

CHAPTER THIRTY-FIVE:

TITLE: DIGITAL ECONOMY COMPANIES WILL NOT FIND THE FLEXIBILITY THEY NEED WITH BPO

A recent feature in Nearshore Americas talked about the huge recent gains for e-commerce and digital economy companies.[1] In the past year these companies have seen an enormous boost because of the Covid-19 pandemic. Many analysts believe that the gains in e-commerce will become permanent because many consumers now prefer to order products online–even if it was their only choice during lockdown.

Data from the U.S. Commerce Department suggests that 2020 sales in online retail grew by 44% on 2019, hitting a value of US$861 billion last year compared to US$598 billion the year before. Canada has grown even faster, registering a hike of 72.7% in online spending – excluding foodservice and catering purchases – this makes Canada the fastest growing e-commerce market on the planet.

All this growth means more pressure from customers on these companies. All that growth is fantastic news, but it does mean that the customer service processes need to keep up, or there will be a detrimental effect on the customer experience.

We were interested to read a comment from the Frost & Sullivan analyst, Sebastian Menutti, Industry Principal for Argentina. Sebastian said: "BPOs leaned a lot on call deflection, automation and AI. Many customers who did not previously leverage those tools began to in 2020 driven by necessity. We have seen a large increase in the demand for bots, intelligent virtual assistants[2] and RPA[3] because they were fundamental in helping BPOs deal with the brisk increase in interactions."

That got us thinking. All the BPOs in this story reported their success in bagging new contracts from e-commerce companies, yet this analyst is saying that one of their key strategies is to deflect the customer from ever reaching the contact center.

Here are a few of our immediate thoughts on this:

1. **Automation will happen, but not like this:** brands do need to get smarter about self-service and automation. You need to think about what customers find when they search Google for help before ever calling. However, intelligent automation should not be used as deflection. If you are deliberately deflecting customers away from ever reaching an agent then your customer service strategy is not flexible enough to cope with your growth.

2. **Flexibility is essential for these companies:** just look at the growth being reported in e-commerce. These companies cannot afford to sign a three year deal with a BPO

that has out of date KPIs after three months. The digital economy needs flexibility at the heart of all services.

3. **There is another way:** We are surprised that the article didn't once reference Gig CX as an option.[4] Take a look back at some of Terry's earlier articles explaining how a Gig CX strategy can build all the flexibility you need into a customer service strategy–certainly enough to handle all the growth a fast-moving e-commerce player will be experiencing.[5]

Let's face it, deflection isn't really a CX strategy, it's a coping mechanism. BPOs take on clients that are growing too fast for them to manage because they want the volume. We understand why–we have all been there. Everyone promises that they can grow as fast as their e-commerce client and then something like Covid-19 happens and turns normal business strategy upside down.

If you want to avoid deflecting customers, if you want all of them to be able to have a great experience each time they interact with your digital economy brand then why not explore some digital economy ideas for managing customer service processes?

CHAPTER THIRTY-SIX:

TITLE: GIG CX WAS A 'WORK FROM ANYWHERE' BEFORE DIGITAL NOMADS ARRIVED

Terry noticed that one of his recent articles was mentioned in a recent feature on the Engage Customer website, commenting on how Gig CX can support an in-house or outsourced contact center.[1] Reading this led Terry to another article on the website talking about the future of the post-pandemic contact center.[2]

It mentioned a normalizing of Gig CX, but also suggested that as work-from-home is also more integrated into both in-house and outsourced customer service processes there will be another important trend–work from anywhere. Once you are no longer tied to an office you can literally hire from anywhere and therefore raise the bar on the people you are hiring to engage with customers.

This Nearshore Americas article suggests one path into the future.[3] Many Caribbean governments are offering fast-track work visas for 'digital nomads'–meaning people who can easily work remotely and therefore only need a laptop and internet connection to work. Many of these countries are traditionally reliant on tourism, but they see a new possibility to attract well-paid residents who want to live and work in a Caribbean paradise.

It's an attractive idea. Imagine if you are at home in a small New York apartment just wishing the summer would arrive faster. You have been working at your shoebox-sized home for over a year now and this experience has proven that your work can continue to be delivered 100% remotely.

Why not just go and spend a year or two on Barbados or the Bahamas instead? Kick back and enjoy the sand, sea, and Caribbean culture and continue to work in the same job. We are sure those dollars also go a lot further down there than they do in downtown Manhattan.

71% of employees at US-startups would like to live overseas if it were possible or allowed in their role.[4] Analysts expect that around 40% of US-based tech jobs will move overseas in the next five years as this idea that digital talent can be sourced from anywhere becomes accepted.

Gig CX is already a part of the "work anywhere" movement.[5] We have long argued that if you want to build a team of customer service representatives then the ability to build your team with people located anywhere creates significant opportunities:

- **Hire fans:** seek out fans of your products and ask those people if they want to help out other customers–build a network of part-time ambassadors
- **Knowledge:** raise the bar and only hire agents who already know about your products. You can't train someone to

understand fashion or support a complex software system inside a week so why not onboard people who already understand what needs to be supported?

- **Commitment:** most contact center agents don't have a lot of commitment to their role–it's just a job and a pay check. The two opportunities mentioned above mean that you can find people who love your products and are committed to your brand–that's a huge difference when compared to a traditional contact center. Wave goodbye to constant attrition. These people actually care.

Compare this the the traditional model of building customer service processes from a contact center. Don't you think you would get better support from some digital nomads who love helping your customers? Does it matter if they have moved to live by a beach?

CHAPTER THIRTY-SEVEN:

TITLE: WOULD YOU WAIT OVER 7 HOURS TO SPEAK TO WALMART?

Note: This chapter is from Terry's perspective.

A couple of weeks ago a friend of mine in Canada sent me this screen grab (image at end of the chapter) from the Walmart customer service page on their phone. The customer is offered the option to either chat to an agent or to call one. The expected wait time for an agent on chat is 7 minutes and for a call it's 7 hours and 15 minutes–good thing it's a toll-free number.

This was in February 2021, not the height of the pandemic chaos last year. Just to convince myself that the service times could really be this bad, I went and checked on the Walmart US help page, to see the time required to call them. It was considerably better than the Canadian example I received, but I was checking in the middle of the day, in the middle of the week, and they still needed about 7 minutes to answer a chat and half an hour to answer a call.

Go back five years and look at how much tolerance people have.[1] If a website didn't load inside 3 seconds then the user would navigate to something else. Today even 3 seconds feels like too long. It loads or it doesn't and you move on.

Loading a website and calling a customer service line for help may feel different, but what do you think is a reasonable time for either? I don't think that half an hour is an acceptable time to wait to speak to a representative of Walmart and seven hours is just off the chart. Even the 7 minutes to start a chat feels like ages when watching your phone, waiting for a response.

Thinking about this as a commentator on the CX industry and looking at the Walmart help pages I noticed several interesting features:

1. **Classic chatbot:** there is the option to be immediately helped by a chatbot, but it has that common problem–it's not very good. It doesn't understand natural language questions very well. Chatbots can work really well for step-by-step processes where the bot is guiding the customer–onboarding a new customer for example–but when the option to ask anything is there then most of them still feel clunky. Plus, if you use the automated chatbot then you are no longer waiting in line for a human.

2. **No asynchronous channel:** if I could send a WhatsApp message then a response in 7 minutes would feel like rapid service. Instead of waiting in line for an agent, I can just fire off a question and then get on with my life–the company can respond as soon as they have someone available. With chat on a standard platform like WhatsApp there is no problem about each message taking a few minutes because it's asynchronous. Why is there no text option?

3. **Covid is no longer an excuse:** to be fair to Walmart, I have not seen the company publicly stating that the Covid-19 pandemic is the reason for this slow service, but I have seen several other major brands doing so. We are now a year into this so no brand should be claiming that they are struggling to answer phone calls because of the pandemic.

As far as I know Walmart processes all their customer service interactions in-house, they don't have a CX specialist managing their contact centers. This leads me to two suggestions:

1. **Consider a CX specialist:** if your internally managed contact centers are performing this poorly then why not see what the CX community can do? Look at the results for companies like Transcom and Teleperformance in 2020–they gained clients, earned more than ever, and managed their way through the pandemic crisis. Agree on some Key Performance Indicators and let the specialists manage these calls.

2. **Explore Gig CX:** Look at our Gig CX book.[2] It's been fascinating to see how Gig CX is growing into one of the most innovative areas of modern CX, supporting work-from-home and finding agents who love the brand. Walmart could retain all their team in-house, but build up a Gig CX bench of talent all across the US–and beyond. Build out the team and just ask them to help out anytime there is an issue. Walmart could even start searching for people who post about the

brand on Instagram and ask, hey do you want to spend a couple of hours a week helping Walmart customers? It could even create a network of Walmart ambassadors, people who already love the company, but now have the opportunity to help the customers.

3. Walmart cannot expect customers to wait hours to offer them help. Loyal customers will drift away to other retailers that actually pick up the phone. Even the biggest and most famous brands can wither and die, especially if you look at how retail is being dramatically changed by the pandemic.

If they want to keep the customer service team in-house then Gig CX has to be worth exploring. If they are open to working with a specialist then I'm sure every major CX supplier would love to win the Walmart contract.

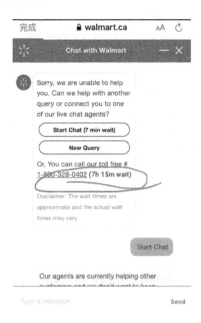

CHAPTER THIRTY-EIGHT:

TITLE: GIG CX CAN CREATE GAINS BY WATCHING THE FX MARKET

One of the key advantages with Gig CX is the ability to hire from anywhere. This has some immediate advantages that can be summarized as:

- **Raise the bar:** if you can search the entire world for talent then you can raise your expectations. You are no longer trying to recruit for a contact center on the edge of town that has to manage with an unreliable bus network. Hire from anywhere and you can choose the best.
- **Find the fans:** why not bring some influencers into your support team? Find your fans on Instagram and ask if they want to get paid to help your customers. You can literally hire fans of your products to talk to and help other customers. Imagine what this can also do for your marketing and visibility–now your fans will love your products even more because they get paid just for talking about them.

- **Resilience:** by widely distributing your customer service function you naturally build resistance into your customer service network. How would a contact center cope with the disruption faced recently in Texas? It's safer to spread the work around the 50 states–and even beyond.

But there is another, more directly financial, advantage that I haven't mentioned before and this is foreign exchange. If you build up a bench of Gig CX agents and they are distributed across both the US and Canada then you can take advantage of currency fluctuations and choose which agents to prioritize.

For example, if you are paying an agent CAD $10 per gig and you are based in the US then at today's rate that's about $7.94. Last year, you could have paid the same person 10 bucks in Canada, but for just $6.90. The rate moves all the time and the Canadian dollar has been depressed recently because of uncertainty over the global oil price.

We are not suggesting that you start dressing like Gordon Gekko[1] and scanning the financial press for hedging options, the foreign exchange advantage comes after all these other benefits of GigCX if you want to rank them by impact, but there certainly is an opportunity. If you can save thousands of dollars a day just by paying more attention to which agents should be prioritized then that has to be useful for your business.

It's just one additional benefit that is available when you start thinking beyond the contact center and exploring Gig CX. Not only can you seek out the best people with deep insight into your products, you can choose where they are located. This can have a direct material impact on your operation, releasing funds that can be used elsewhere in the business–or just creating much-needed savings from operational costs.

CHAPTER THIRTY-NINE:

TITLE: GIG CX CAN COMPLEMENT YOUR CONTACT CENTER, NOT REPLACE IT

At the end of 2020, Terry was delighted to receive an invitation to appear as a guest on the CX Files podcast.[1] The industry analyst Peter Ryan was the host and as you might expect, he grilled Terry on the opportunities presented by Gig CX and what LiveXchange plans for 2021.[2]

We would like to repeat one of the themes that Peter covered during that interview. Peter was asking about the future of contact centers as we emerge from the Covid-19 crisis. The centers all had to send their people home so there is a question that the Business Process Outsourcing (BPO) companies could all ask–why do we need these people to be doing 8-hour shifts 5 days a week when we could switch to a gig model?

It's a fair point, but this is one of the confusions we often hear when people ask about Gig CX. It is more flexible than a traditional contact center and you can ramp up and down more easily to handle seasonality, but we don't expect that Gig CX will be a widespread replacement for contact centers. These companies have so much invested in their existing model that we don't think any of them will want to see Gig CX as a direct replacement for what they do–however it can be used to complement their processes.

This can work in multiple ways, for example:

- A BPO works with LiveXchange to train up a bench of talent to support a specific client–they can step in to help out anytime a seasonal boost is needed and then released after, so the core contact center team continues as normal.
- A client hires a BPO to manage the core of their customer service processes from their contact center, but also uses the LiveXchange system to build their own bench of talent that can be deployed whenever needed–in parallel with the BPO team. Like an insurance policy to always be ready to help the BPO.
- Either a BPO, or the end client, hires LiveXchange to not just supply the Gig CX platform, but also to manage the recruitment process–so the end client or the BPO can ask us to step in to help with seasonal peaks. We can help and you don't even need to worry about managing the system–let us handle it.

This is the real value of Gig CX. We can work with the end client or the contact center–it really doesn't matter. We can just supply the platform or we can handle the entire process.

Either way, you get your core contact center team there each day covering off the regular call volume, but anytime a peak is approaching we can quickly scale up and manage it with gig workers based at home. As soon as the crisis is gone, we remove or reduce the available gigs.

It might be that some companies and executives are entirely comfortable with the gig model and do choose to build a complete customer service solution this way, but it's not what we are expecting in the near future. Manage your regular call volume with your contact center team or BPO and add a Gig CX component to your customer service processes.

The answer isn't hiring seasonal workers, even though that's what every BPO business journal suggests.[3] What else would they say? They are in the business of growing contact centers, but they can't handle huge seasonal spikes. How would you accommodate everyone anyway if you had to double the volume of calls handled just for a week?

Think smart and think Gig CX. You can work with us as a BPO, or an end client that would usually hire a BPO. We can manage the processes, or you can just take our platform. Either way, you can manage customer expectations and continue to deliver great service without the chaos of a temporary recruitment drive or the pain of training people to just let them go after managing a spike.

CHAPTER FORTY:

TITLE: HOW GIG CX CAN BUILD FLEXIBILITY INTO YOUR BPO SOLUTION

One of the themes we have often written about in these pages is that Gig CX is not a replacement for Business Process Outsourcing (BPO) and contact center specialists.[1] We don't see any immediate future where the companies that have deep expertise in designing and building customer service strategies will just be replaced by Gig CX.

However, there is an enormous opportunity for the BPO companies to work with Gig CX as a platform that can improve the service they offer to their own clients.

Terry knows that one of the main challenges he always faced when he was working for a major customer service specialist was seasonality–those peak periods in the year when your contact center is slammed. Business spikes, customer satisfaction plummets, because you just can't handle all the customer calls, and it just doesn't work for anyone. The team is stressed and the customers are annoyed.

This always happens because contact centers have a physical limit. You can't just squeeze more people into the building and even if you are working with some work-from-home (WFH) resource then they are still working to the same shift patterns as the center. It's still not very flexible even with the WFH resource.

This is where we see a major opportunity for BPO companies to partner with Gig CX specialists such as LiveXchange. Consider these ideas:

- You can tap into a pool of **trained resource whenever you need it**–just make the shifts available and control what you need to the nearest half-hour shift.
- **You can ramp down immediately** as soon as the rush is over.
- **You are working with people who are trained**, know the client and their products, and in many cases may know the products far better than the agents in your contact center if you have taken care to select people who really love the brand.
- **You maintain full control** of the entire gig operation–we are providing a platform that allows you to build your own CX solution in the same way that Salesforce doesn't tell you how to manage your CRM.
- You can tap into our **cloud-based technology platform**, which may even make it far easier for you to facilitate your own WFH integration.

These are the key points. BPOs don't need to be hiring temporary workers, training them and then laying them off after a seasonal peak. Build up a bench of gig workers who are always available.

You might have a seasonal rush or you might have a surprise-whatever happens you can tap into this trained resource through the Gig CX platform.

Most importantly, you are buying access to a platform, a tool, that allows you to build flexibility into your contact center operation. Black Friday should never again be a period where you need to ramp up and train new team members over weeks or months-you can just switch on the extra talent as needed.

CHAPTER FORTY-ONE:

TITLE: WHY WORK IN A CONTACT CENTER WHEN THE GOVERNMENT IS GIVING AWAY $2,000?

The CARES Act is a $2.2 trillion economic stimulus bill.[1] It was hastily created back in March 2020 when it became clear that the American economy was going to be hammered by the Covid-19 pandemic. The package of measures was designed to help anyone affected by the pandemic, from healthcare providers, to businesses, and also individuals. We did get hammered, so this has been a lifeline for many.

You may have been lucky enough to receive one of the $2,000 checks mailed out recently.[2] Congress had originally agreed to send individuals $600 as part of a direct stimulus package where the government puts cash into the hands of citizens so they can kick-start the economy. Fortunately for the American people, there was an election recently and both the presidential candidates said they would raise the number to $2,000 instead.

Free money. That has to be good news, right?

Of course, a lot of people have seen their job or business struggling during this crisis and we hope they get all the help they need to get moving again, but the stimulus checks are causing problems for some companies where people have been working throughout the crisis.

Let's be a little more specific. We have been hearing from several people all over the country that contact centers are seeing a wave of resignations. Far more people are leaving their jobs–and it is often because of money.

Think about it this way. A contact center agent is getting $12-13 per hour and working maybe 37.5 hours a week. Multiply that out to get a monthly figure and it's just over $2,000–before taxes. A lot of agents are looking at the free stimulus check and asking why then can get this for free from the government and yet they need to work hard for a month to take home less.

It's not the fault of the individual contact centers. The competition is cutthroat so they all need to keep costs down and we can understand how some of those agents must be feeling. Imagine if you had worked through this pandemic only to find that your monthly salary is less than the cash Congress is giving away free as stimulus cash? It doesn't really inspire anyone to head back in for another shift. Anyone who was already dissatisfied or thinking about leaving might tip over the edge and email their resignation.

We don't want to see our BPO friends struggling because agents are leaving their jobs. We all worked in the contact center business for years so we know what it's like when the pressure is on. As Terry said in a recent article, I want to show my BPO buddies that Gig CX is on their side.[3]

If your attrition is high at present, triggered by the stimulus checks or anything else, then why not try partnering with LiveXchange? We can help you build up a team of Gig CX agents that love talking to customers. You can simply augment your existing team with a Gig CX team–this is not an either/or proposition. We will make your team stronger, not replace them. Some recently departed employees might even come back on board if they can work on a gig basis–and take home a lot more each month.

Work with us. Gig CX isn't out to destroy BPO, we want to help you through this rough patch. Let us help you steer a path through to the recovery. A new normal is waiting and Gig CX can help you get there.

CHAPTER FORTY-TWO:

TITLE: GIG CX WILL NOT REPLACE CONTACT CENTERS—BUT IT CAN IMPROVE THEM!

One of the common misconceptions about Gig CX is that those of us who evangelize the concept are always looking to replace the traditional contact center. This is far from the truth. Terry spent many years working for one of the leading global customer experience suppliers with contact centers in 80 countries. We are not proposing that Gig CX is a direct replacement for this entire industry.

There truth is that there are at least three areas where we believe that Gig CX really shines and offers a new opportunity that can really help contact center operators:

1. **The replacement of an internal customer service process:** if you manage your customer service processes in-house and struggle with the physical need for a contact center, the technology and regulatory requirements, and the constant need to hire and train new agents then why

not just consider how your contact center might work in the cloud?

2. **Augmenting in-house customer service:** if you are comfortable with your in-house service center, but struggle when new products are launched or at certain times of the year–for example the holiday season or Black Friday–then you could just augment the team by having some Gig CX resource on standby for when you need to ramp up.

3. **Augmenting a Business Process Outsourcing supplier:** this is where a customer service specialist is providing contact center services to their clients, but they can then add Gig CX capability to their offer to dramatically increase their ability to ramp up and down. Instead of worrying about how to get more people into a physical contact center for Black Friday, add to the team by building a Gig CX layer on top of your regular team.

When you look at Gig CX from this angle there is the potential for it to be a useful tool for managers who run their own in-house customer service center or those who work with a supplier and find that their supplier constantly struggles during those periods when they need to stretch.

It's not a solution to ban overtime and ask everyone to just work harder. Many companies face peak periods where demand can increase to be many multiples of regular demand. Think about sports teams releasing tickets for games or concert promoters announcing popular shows. We know we can't visit any of these events right now, but they will be back.

A contact center handling sports events can require 30x the normal coverage when a major event goes on sale–you are not going to handle this kind of demand by just asking the team to work through their lunch break. Whether you are working with a BPO supplier or managing your CX processes in-house, there is a strong reason for you to explore Gig CX.

We are not out to replace contact centers, we want to make them better. It's not Gig CX or BPO it's Gig CX and BPO.

CHAPTER FORTY-THREE:

TITLE: GIGCX AND BPO— LET'S WORK TOGETHER!

What are the most common problems that every Business Process Outsourcing (BPO) company and contact center has to manage? We know that every different manager will list them in a different order, but based on our own experience working in contact centers, here are the key challenges from our point of view:

1. **Attrition:** the ongoing need to hire and train agents because you know that the contact center is never stable. A center with 500 agents might need to hire and train over 40 new people every month just to stand still.

2. **Managing CSAT:** the constant need to keep customer satisfaction levels high.

3. **Managing ESAT:** agents need to be engaged, yet they might not care at all for the insurance policies they are supporting. How do you constantly improve employee satisfaction when they might only be there for the cash?

4. **Technology Creep:** new systems are added, new clients use different systems, and and it can end up like a spaghetti of systems where the agents can only make it all work by using cut and paste.

5. **Boosting Performance:** the constant battle to keep improving performance.

6. **Constant Training And Reminders:** agents forget details about products and services they may not be familiar with, but they need to support. How do they remember if they don't really care?

7. **Concentration:** keeping agents focused and performing consistently throughout their entire shift, not just at the start of the day.

8. **Peak demand periods:** Typical advice in the industry suggests improving your forecasting, hiring more agents, and improving your training. This is all good general advice, but it will never be good enough if you face peak periods where demand for service increases several times– Black Friday weekend for example.[1]

Meanwhile, contrast all of these problems with Gig CX. You don't have an attrition problem because you are hiring people who love the brands they are supporting and this feeds directly into both CSAT and ESAT. You have all your systems in the cloud so they are more easily updated and improved. You don't need to worry about performance and concentration because, once again, you have hired people who enjoy working with the brands they are supporting and they are not forced to work full-day shifts. If they want to just do an hour, that's fine.

But most of all, the problem of how to manage peak periods is entirely different when using Gig CX because you have no constraints on how many agents you make available to help customers during these periods of peak demand. Your only constraint is the need to plan ahead so enough people are trained and ready to go.

For all these reasons, we believe there is an enormous opportunity for existing BPO companies to partner with Gig CX providers, such as LiveXchange. We are not going to eat your lunch or steal your business, but you can certainly improve the service you deliver to your own clients by adding a Gig CX layer.

Imagine the ability to build a flexible group of Gig CX agents into your delivery model so you can always ramp up when needed–and down again immediately. These agents don't have a problem concentrating and don't need close supervision or performance boosting management. They will choose to work with the brands they like working with.

BPO and contact center specialists have always struggled with peaks, but as we listed, there are many other ongoing issues they all need to manage. Finding a Gig CX partner could help resolve many of these challenges–and fast.

CHAPTER FORTY-FOUR:

TITLE: GIG CX ALLOWS YOU TO BUILD AN ARMY OF FANS FOR YOUR BRAND

We are often asked to explain Gig CX in the context of the contact center. A traditional customer service operation requires a large building full of customer service agents who all need to live close enough to the center to be able to commute there each day, and they will generally work a full day on each shift.

Gig CX is very different, not least because you can be more flexible about the shifts so it's much easier to ramp your cover up and down as needed. Obviously there is no need for the contact center building as well, because the contact center is virtual and only exists in the cloud.

But there is a really important difference that we think is often missed when we just talk about these comparisons to a contact center.

Companies that hire people to work in a contact center want them to be nearby, to have good communication skills, and to work on the service processes for whatever clients the contact center works with.

This can be turned upside down with Gig CX. You can hire people from anywhere and this means that you can actively seek people who really love your products. You are not focusing on their ability to speak to customers–that can easily be trained–you are focusing on finding the people who already love your brand and your products.

We cannot emphasize how important this is and how different it is to the contact center agent who will apply for a customer service job and not know if they are going to be allocated into a role with a bank or a retailer.

Let's say you are a retail brand focused on women's fashion. How cool would it be if the people on your service team actually love your clothes, so when customers call or send a message, they get a response from someone who really loves the product and is completely focused on fixing the issue?

It's simple. Go to Instagram and find all the people who are posting about your clothes and ask if they want to be brand ambassadors. They can actually get paid to get closer to a brand they already love–they are posting photos all over their social networks already!

What about if you just published a game on the Apple and Google App Stores? People are downloading it to their phones all over the world and a few click on the HELP button–maybe they got locked out of the game. Why not find some of the gamers who already love your game and ask them if they want to earn some extra cash by helping other gamers when they are not playing it themselves?

The power of this approach is obvious to us, but we feel that when analysts compare Gig CX to Business Process Outsourcing and contact centers they really miss the power of hiring brand ambassadors to handle your customer service processes. We are sure that when a CX expert like Stephen Lloyd[1] is calling the Red Sox[2] to find out about their social distancing policies he would rather talk to another fan rather than a robot!

The advantage of this approach does not stop just with the improved experience of customers interacting with fans of the brand. If you are a fashion brand and you want promotion then what's the twenty-first century approach? Work with your influencer community–send them some free gifts and new products.

What if you already have hundreds of micro-influencers already working for you, directly helping your customers? The power of this network is multiplied–you are not just sending them a few free gifts, they love your brand and now they are earning real cash by helping other customers. Their social posts will probably explode with even more photos featuring your products–especially if you send a few freebies to high-performers.

Let me know about other examples or areas where you think that working with ambassadors for your brand would be far more powerful than using a contact center–the list could certainly go on!

CHAPTER FORTY-FIVE:

TITLE: GIGCX CAN HELP YOU ACE YOUR SEASONAL PEAKS

Seasonality is a well known issue in retail. Valentine's Day, Mother's Day, the back-to-school season, Halloween, Black Friday, and the Christmas and Hanukkah holidays all create peaks in demand for different types of retailer and they all have to find different ways of coping with the stress that a peak period places on their customer service team.

But seasonality isn't just restricted to retail. As you might expect, the travel industry also has very distinct peaks and troughs, particularly for tourism. Sports and events, such as concerts, usually have very specific seasons. Businesses focused on health, such as gyms, often peak early in the year. Peaks can also be created by new products, rather than any specific season–if a celebrity wears a certain item of clothing they it might suddenly be in much more demand.

Peaks in demand usually lead to a peak in the requirement for customer service interactions. It could be because many more items are being returned or exchanged or just because the increased interest leads to many more questions and enquiries.

How do you cope with this? How do you prepare your contact center to manage a weekend like Black Friday where you might see the same business in a weekend that normally covers an entire month?

Preparation, training, and hiring in some temporary cover are many of the tips you will see in the contact center journals. These are great tips if you are expecting a 25% increase in customer interactions, but what if your seasonal peak leads to a 500% per cent increase in demand on your contact center?

This is where Gig CX can be an important tool in your customer service strategy. You don't need to expand the physical contact center because the agents will all work remotely from home, connected to a virtual contact center. You can plan in advance and ensure that the agents are trained and ready, but more importantly you can target who you want on your team because the best people to hire will be your existing fans.

Scan the social networks to find which customers are talking about your products. Who is writing reviews or creating unboxing videos? Ask these people directly if they would like some flexible work supporting your products and you might be pleasantly surprised by the response.

Many of these online influencers will love the opportunity to help your customers because they already love the brand. To many of them it's just great to experience that recognition from your brand and it's a bonus to get paid each time they help a customer.

Now, build a pool of these influencers who are trained how to manage customer service interactions and security-cleared to access the systems. They don't want or expect work everyday, but you can tap into this deep pool of resource anytime you know there will be a seasonal rush.

Alert the group in advance, hey we need at least 100 people to cover these hours over Black Friday–is anyone in?

Suddenly, your contact center will be able to cope with a peak period not by hiring in temps who only want to see the end of a shift. You can have a team of expert influencers–who love your products–helping out during your busiest and most stressful periods.

These people don't need employee engagement programs, you are only going to call on people who are already interested in your brand. You are offering them payment for their help, but you can throw in the bonus of recognition from a brand they love. Maybe even send some free gifts to the best on the team–you know they are going to end up on Instagram.

This is how to manage seasonality and peak periods. Don't just cope, make your peaks the best time of the year, when the Gig CX influencers ride to the rescue!

CHAPTER FORTY-SIX:

DON'T FEAR THE GIGCX AGENT—THEY ALSO LOVE YOUR CUSTOMERS!

Before the Covid-19 pandemic there was a common fear amongst customer service executives that if their agents worked from home then quality, productivity, and security would all be at risk. The pandemic demonstrated that none of the work from home disasters they expected need to be true.

It's possible to deliver a robust customer service strategy for major brands with all the agents working from home. Look around—every single company managing contact centers is doing it right now because of Covid-19.

This has led to a dramatic increase in opportunities for GixCX. If you are going to design a customer service strategy that has all your agents working from home then why would you build your management processes to reflect how they worked inside an office? For example, 8-hour shifts and being paid for a shift regardless of productivity?

GigCX embraces the possibility to work anywhere, but it goes far beyond the office workers that have been sent home because of the pandemic.

GigCX allows you far more flexibility over when people are working and for how long. You can schedule shifts that the agents then sign up for and this can be controlled down to the nearest half an hour. You can also focus on rewarding agents for each time they help a customer–pay them based on results, not time.

GigCX facilitates this change in approach, but we can sense that some executives are unsure about the gig economy in customer service because they feel that in-house agents must be better or more reliable.

We think this is just a change in approach, a mindset shift. What makes a great customer service agent? Usually it's their ability to communicate and their knowledge of the products they are supporting. Once you can go national (or even international) with your recruitment then you can ensure that you select agents who love your brand and actively want to support your customers.

Agents recruited this way–to specifically work from home–are generally older than those working in a contact center. They have more experience of the products they are supporting and life in general. They are more likely to value the flexibility of GigCX and actively want to choose when they can work more hours and when they can take a day off. GigCX attrition is dramatically lower than that seen in contact centers because these agents want to work flexibly from home. They like their job.

So GigCX means you can access more experienced and knowledgable agents, but what about security, training and quality?

Our technology ensures that only known agents can login and access customer data. We believe that our systems are even more secure than most security systems deployed inside office environments. Many security breaches are inside jobs and which agents are a bigger threat–the ones who love the flexibility their job provides or the ones staring at a clock in a contact center?

GigCX agents are remotely trained for each new account they plan to work with and refresher training is applied as needed. Our training was always designed to be delivered remotely and is not just re-packaged slides from an earlier training course that used to be delivered in a contact center.

Quality is always monitored and because you are directly managing the agents using our system you have complete control over the metrics and how agents are managing your customers–there is no account manager or business process outsourcing company in the middle that needs to be managed.

At the end of the day one of the major advantages of building a GigCX solution is not just the increase in productivity and efficiency, but the fact that you are hiring agents who actively want to be working from home. They want the flexibility that GigCX offers them. They want to be supporting customers in brands they enjoy working with. They don't quit at 100%+ attrition levels because these agents are building their work around their lifestyle–they want to do this.

Contrast this to the difficulties many contact centers have when engaging their employees. You can wear funny hats and decorate the office in bright colors, but if they are really just there for the pay check then don't expect any loyalty and don't expect unengaged agents to deliver a great customer experience.

GigCX is about more than just flexibility. It's about finding people who really want to engage with your customers. Don't fear GigCX agents–it's highly likely that they will love your customers far more than any agent in a traditional contact center ever would!

REFERENCES:

Chapter One: Could The Great Resignation Be A Great Opportunity For Your Business?

1. https://www.thehrdirector.com/great-resignation-become-great-retention/
2. https://hbr.org/2021/09/who-is-driving-the-great-resignation
3. https://www.cnbc.com/2021/11/01/great-resignation-may-be-altering-workforce-dynamic-for-good.html

Chapter Two: Do 4-Day Weeks Prove That More Hours Is Not More Productivity?

1. https://www.linkedin.com/in/terry-rybolt-808361/detail/recent-activity/posts/
2. https://www.bbc.com/news/business-59377940
3. https://www.atombank.co.uk/

Chapter Three: Customer Service Representatives Are The Most In-Demand Workers In The USA In 2021

1. https://www.washingtonpost.com/business/2021/11/12/job-quit-september-openings/

2. https://lensa.com/insights/
   the-lensa-index/

3. https://www.npr.org/2021/10/28/
   1049980529/starbucks-and-costco-
   raising-wages-in-the-nationwide-
   competition-for-workers

Chapter Four: GigCX Can Change The Debate About The Future Of Work

1. https://news.bloomberglaw.com/daily-
   labor-report/gig-economy-rise-prompts-
   ftc-chiefs-call-to-alter-antitrust-law

2. https://www.latimes.com/business/
   technology/story/2021-08-25/
   after-prop-22-ruling-whats-next-uber-lyft

3. https://lensa.com/insights/
   the-lensa-index/

Chapter Five: Talent-as-a-Service Becomes A Reality As Freelancers Become The US Majority

1. http://www.youtube.com/
   watch?v=m7NChV93LBw

2. https://www.statista.
   com/statistics/921593/
   gig-economy-number-of-freelancers-us/

3. https://yfsmagazine.com/2021/10/13/
   what-every-ceo-should-know-
   about-talent-as-a-service/

Chapter Six: HfS Research Says 'Get Ready For Gig CX!'

1. https://www.linkedin.com/in/
   terry-rybolt-808361/recent-activity/posts/

2. https://www.hfsresearch.com/research/
the-biggest-operational-model-shift-
is-just-ahead-get-ready-for-gig/

Chapter Seven: Can You Serve All Your Extra Customers In The Post-Covid Boom?

1. https://chainstoreage.com/
apparel-spending-expected-soar-q4
2. https://internetretailing.net/
international/490bn-of-in-store-
sales-moved-online-globally-in-2021-
as-cross-border-takes-off-23880
3. https://www.upwork.com/documents/
freelance-forward-2020

Chapter Eight: Gig CX Offers What Workers Want Most–Flexibility

1. https://www.theguardian.com/
film/2021/sep/28/the-gig-is-up-
documentary-gig-workers-economy
2. https://hbswk.hbs.edu/item/how-much-
is-freedom-worth-for-gig-workers-a-lot
3. https://myworkchoice.com/blog/
whats-causing-turnover-in-your-call-center

Chapter Nine: Ensuring Your WFH Agents Are Secure Needs More Than Just Thin Clients

1. https://livexchange.com/
how-we-do-it-livexchange/security/

Chapter Ten: How Has The Great Resignation Affected Your Industry?

1. https://apnews.com/article/business-lifestyle-new-york-306596169aed48d6d7bebe351ce51ad0

2. https://www.mckinsey.com/business-functions/people-and-organizational-performance/our-insights/great-attrition-or-great-attraction-the-choice-is-yours

3. https://www.npr.org/2021/10/22/1048332481/the-great-resignation-why-people-are-leaving-their-jobs-in-growing-numbers

4. https://www.forbes.com/sites/jessicalin/2021/10/20/meet-the-startup-turning-customers-into-next-gen-customer-service-for-brands-they-love/

Chapter Eleven: Could Gig CX Be The Answer To The Great Resignation?

1.https://fortune.com/2021/08/26/pandemic-burnout-career-changes-great-resignation-adobe/

1. https://www.entrepreneur.com/article/383109

2. https://tearsheet.co/payments/gig-workers-are-paving-the-future-of-payments/

Chapter Twelve: Gig Workers Are Calling Time On The Monthly Salary Check

1. https://chainstoreage.com/higher-wages-could-lead-more-inflation-warns-nrf-economist

2. https://hbr.org/2021/09/
   who-is-driving-the-great-resignation
3. https://www.forbes.com/sites/hollycorbett/
   2021/07/28/the-great-resignation-why-
   employees-dont-want-to-go-back-to-the-
   office/
4. https://payshark.com/
5. https://tearsheet.co/payments/
   gig-workers-are-paving-the-
   future-of-payments/

Chapter Thirteen: Walmart Launches Nationwide Delivery Service In The US

1. https://www.cbsnews.com/news/
   walmart-golocal-delivery-services-
   small-businesses-two-hours/
2. https://www.reuters.com/world/
   us/exclusive-us-labor-secretary-
   says-most-gig-workers-should-
   be-classified-2021-04-29

Chapter Fourteen: Black Friday Hopes And Fears Are Here Again

1. https://www.advantagecall.com/blog/
   prepare-early-scaling-up-your-customer-
   care-for-black-friday-cyber-monday-2021
2. https://www.amazon.com/
   GigCX-Customer-Service-
   Twenty-First-Century-ebook/
   dp/B08MB1G9BD/
3. https://cxfiles.libsyn.com/gigcx-
   discussion-featuring-mckinsey-
   livexchange-and-newage-products

4. https://www.forbes.com/sites/ kirimasters/2021/09/07/retail- brands-gear-up-for-second- shippageddon/?sh=1517efda358e

5. https://www.reuters.com/world/ us/exclusive-us-labor-secretary- says-most-gig-workers-should- be-classified-2021-04-29/

6. https://www.intelligentsourcing.net/ gig-cx-debate-who-is-really-using- the-gig-economy-in-cx-and-why/

Chapter Fifteen: We Need A New Way To Think About Measuring Work And Performance

1. https://hbr.org/2020/07/ remote-managers-are-having-trust-issues

2. https://www.washingtonpost. com/technology/2020/04/30/ work-from-home-surveillance/

3. https://ieeexplore.ieee.org/ abstract/document/807960

Chapter Eighteen: Building A Gig Mindset Means Changing How We View Work

1. https://www.amazon.com/Gig-Mindset- Reclaim-Reinvent-Disruption-ebook/ dp/B082QN2DJ6/

2. https://www.linkedin.com/ company/mural.co/

3. https://www.amazon.com/4-Hour- Work-Week-Escape-Anywhere-ebook/ dp/B006X0M2TS/

4. https://slate.com/business/2021/06/
   workers-quitting-jobs-woohoo.html

Chapter Nineteen: Employers And Employees Both Want Flexibility, So Let's Build It!

1. https://www.linkedin.com/pulse/
   dont-fear-gigcx-agent-also-love-
   your-customers-terry-rybolt/

Chapter Twenty: A Million Americans Quit Their Job In June–Why?

1. https://www.fitchratings.com/research/
   infrastructure-project-finance/fitch-
   revises-us-air-traffic-assumptions-
   upward-for-airlines-airports-12-07-2021

2. https://www.cnbc.com/2021/07/10/
   mcdonalds-minimum-wage-raise-and-
   the-fast-food-franchise-future-.html

3. https://www.forbes.com/sites/
   tomspiggle/2021/07/08/what-does-a-
   worker-want-what-the-labor-shortage-
   really-tells-us/?sh=6d354b23539d

4. https://cxfiles.libsyn.com/gigcx-
   discussion-featuring-mckinsey-
   livexchange-and-newage-products

Chapter Twenty-One: The Gig Economy Cannot Be Ignored–People Want Flexibility

1. https://www.reuters.com/world/
   us/exclusive-us-labor-secretary-
   says-most-gig-workers-should-
   be-classified-2021-04-29/

2. https://en.wikipedia.org/
   wiki/2020_California_Proposition_22

3. https://www.forbes.com/sites/
    tomspiggle/2021/07/08/what-
    does-a-worker-want-what-the-
    labor-shortage-really-tells-us/

Chapter Twenty-Two: WFH Security Requires More Than Just Firewalls

1. https://blog.invoiced.com/what-
    is-pci-level-1-compliance-and-
    why-do-you-need-to-know

Chapter Twenty-Three: The Global Talent Crunch Means That Jobs Need To Be Redefined

1. https://www.reuters.com/world/the-great-
    reboot/swiss-bank-ubs-allow-most-staff-
    adopt-hybrid-working-2021-06-28/
2. https://www.kornferry.com/content/
    dam/kornferry/docs/pdfs/KF-Future-
    of-Work-Talent-Crunch-Report.pdf

Chapter Twenty-Four: Tackling Seasonality Head-On With GigCX

1. https://cxfiles.libsyn.com/gigcx-
    discussion-featuring-mckinsey-
    livexchange-and-newage-products
2. https://www.linkedin.com/in/
    mahesh-raghuram-8600a726/

Chapter Twenty-Five: #GigCX: LiveXchange Featured On The CX Files Podcast

1. https://cxfiles.libsyn.com/gigcx-
    discussion-featuring-mckinsey-
    livexchange-and-newage-products

2. https://www.linkedin.com/in/mahesh-raghuram-8600a726/

3. https://www.linkedin.com/in/vinay-gupta-b3028a16/

4. https://www.linkedin.com/in/markhillary/

5. https://www.linkedin.com/pulse/gigcx-can-help-you-ace-your-seasonal-peaks-terry-rybolt/

Chapter Twenty-Six: WFH Alliance Delivers A Strong Boost To WFH Culture

1. https://www.linkedin.com/feed/update/urn:li:activity:6813101847348359168/

2. https://hbr.org/podcast/2021/06/hybrid-work-is-here-to-stay-now-what

Chapter Twenty-Seven: Industry Disruptors Need Disruptive Ideas To Manage CX

1. https://www.cnbc.com/2021/05/25/these-are-the-2021-cnbc-disruptor-50-companies.html

2. https://www.cnbc.com/2021/05/25/robinhood-disruptor-50.html

3. https://www.cnbc.com/2021/01/28/robinhood-interactive-brokers-restrict-trading-in-gamestop-s.html

4. https://www.cnbc.com/2021/05/25/stripe-disruptor-50.html

5. https://brand-minds.medium.com/why-did-kodak-fail-and-what-can-you-learn-from-its-failure-70b92793493c

6. https://newsroom.spotify.com/2021-02-22/
spotify-expands-international-footprint-
bringing-audio-to-80-new-markets/

7. https://www.amazon.com/
GigCX-Customer-Service-
Twenty-First-Century-ebook/
dp/B08MB1G9BD/

Chapter Twenty-Eight: Building A Gig CX Advocacy Network Enhances Both CX AND Diversity

1. https://www.linkedin.com/pulse/
how-gig-cx-can-build-flexibility-
your-bpo-solution-terry-rybolt/

Chapter Twenty-Nine: IRS Customer Service Is So Bad Forbes Called It 'Dire' In A Headline

1. https://www.forbes.com/sites/
sarahhansen/2021/04/26/
with-delayed-may-17-tax-filing-
deadline-approaching-these-10-
numbers-sum-up-the-dire-backlog-at-
the-irs-and-its-impact-on-taxpayers/

2. http://j.mp/gigcx

Chapter Thirty: Gig CX Is Different To The Gig Economy Lawmakers Understand

1. https://www.gartner.com/en/human-
resources/research/talentneuron/
gig-economy

2. https://www.pewresearch.org/fact-
tank/2018/04/11/millennials-largest-
generation-us-labor-force/

3. https://www.upwork.com/press/releases/freelance-misconceptions
4. https://www.businessinsider.com/salesforce-employees-can-work-from-home-permanently-2021-2
5. https://www.latimes.com/business/technology/story/2020-02-03/uber-ab5-driver-app

Chapter Thirty-One: The TSA Is Preparing For A Summer Boom In Travel–Is Your CX Ready?

1. https://www.washingtonpost.com/transportation/2021/04/28/tsa-hiring/
2. https://www.flightglobal.com/jobs/most-commercial-pilots-no-longer-flying/142026.article
3. https://www.stuff.co.nz/business/120891348/coronavirus-virgin-australia-pilots-picking-onions-stacking-supermarket-shelves-after-layoffs

Chapter Thirty-Two: Gig CX Can Help You Engage Earlier With Customers

1. 1.https://www.bellinghamherald.com/news/coronavirus/article251076309.html
2. https://www.voanews.com/a/covid-19-pandemic_one-year-after-closing-us-canada-border-remains-closed/6202740.html
3. https://travel.gc.ca/travel-covid

Chapter Thirty-Three: BPOs Serving Agile Customers In The Digital Economy Need The Flexibility Of Gig CX

1. https://nearshoreamericas.com/ ecommerce-retail-digital-economy-bpo-rethink/

Chapter Thirty-Four: How Do You Build A Flexible Contact Center If You Don't Want To Use Outsourcing?

1. https://books.google.com.br/books/ about/Competing_for_the_Future.html
2. https://www.forbes.com/sites/ theyec/2021/03/19/five-tips-for-outsourcing-business-processes-effectively-in-2021/
3. https://www.amazon.com/ GigCX-Customer-Service-Twenty-First-Century-ebook/ dp/B08MB1G9BD/
4. https://livexchange.com/how-we-do-it/

Chapter Thirty-Five: Digital Economy Companies Will Not Find The Flexibility They Need With BPO

1. https://nearshoreamericas. com/ecommerce-retail-digital-economy-bpo-rethink/
2. https://nearshoreamericas. com/unisys-offering-next-gen-development-tools-for-free/
3. https://nearshoreamericas.com/ rpa-vendor-uipath-worth-us35-billion/

4. https://www.amazon.com/
   GigCX-Customer-Service-
   Twenty-First-Century-ebook/
   dp/B08MB1G9BD/
5. https://www.linkedin.com/pulse/
   gigcx-can-help-you-ace-your-
   seasonal-peaks-terry-rybolt/

Chapter Thirty-Six: Gig CX Was a 'Work From Anywhere' Before Digital Nomads Arrived

1. https://engagecustomer.com/
   gigcx-is-rewriting-the-rules-on-how-
   to-design-a-contact-centre/
2. https://engagecustomer.com/
   what-is-the-future-of-the-post-
   pandemic-contact-centre/
3. https://nearshoreamericas.com/
   digital-nomad-visas-caribbean/
4. https://www.businessinsider.com/71-
   us-tech-employees-move-abroad-
   work-remotely-2020-8?r=MX&IR=T
5. https://www.amazon.com/
   GigCX-Customer-Service-
   Twenty-First-Century-ebook/
   dp/B08MB1G9BD/

Chapter Thirty-Seven: Would You Wait Over 7 Hours To Speak To Walmart?

1. https://www.bbc.com/news/
   business-37100091
2. https://www.amazon.com/GigCX-Customer-
   Service-Twenty-First-Century-ebook/dp/
   B08MB1G9BD/

Chapter Thirty-Eight: Gig CX Can Create Gains By Watching The FX Market

1. http://www.youtube.com/watch?v=6DaltDKFfno

Chapter Thirty-Nine: Gig CX Can Complement Your Contact Center, Not Replace It

1. https://cxfiles.libsyn.com/terry-rybolt-livexchange-cx-the-gig-economy-gigcx

2. https://www.linkedin.com/in/peter-ryan-montreal/

3. https://www.dizzion.com/resource/blog/how-call-centers-deal-with-the-holiday-rush/

Chapter Forty: How Gig CX Can Build Flexibility Into Your BPO Solution

1. https://www.linkedin.com/pulse/gigcx-bpo-lets-work-together-terry-rybolt/

Chapter Forty-One: Why Work In A Contact Center When The Government Is Giving Away $2,000?

1. https://en.wikipedia.org/wiki/CARES_Act

2. https://edition.cnn.com/2021/01/14/politics/stimulus-payments-2000-dollars-biden/index.html

3. https://www.linkedin.com/pulse/gigcx-bpo-lets-work-together-terry-rybolt/

Chapter Forty-Three: GigCX And BPO–Let's Work Together!

1. https://fonolo.com/blog/2019/06/how-to-prepare-your-call-center-for-cyber-monday-and-black-friday-tip-sheet/

Chapter Forty-Four: Gig CX Allows You To Build An Army Of Fans For Your Brand

1. https://www.linkedin.com/in/stephenloynd/
2. https://www.mlb.com/redsox

APPENDIX 1:

THE CX FILES PODCAST—JUNE 25, 2021

THE GIGCX DISCUSSION

In this episode of the CX Files podcast, Mark Hillary led a discussion focused on GigCX with several guests.

The guests were:

Vinay Gupta, Senior Expert, McKinsey & Company

https://www.mckinsey.com/
https://www.linkedin.com/in/vinay-gupta-b3028a16/

Terry Rybolt, Chief Revenue Officer, LiveXchange

https://livexchange.com/
https://www.linkedin.com/in/terry-rybolt-808361/

Mahesh Raghuram, Director of Customer Service, NewAge Products

https://newageproducts.com/ca/
https://www.linkedin.com/in/mahesh-raghuram-8600a726/

Search for 'CX Files' on your preferred podcast app and scroll back through the episodes to listen to the complete episode or use this link to listen online:

https://cxfiles.libsyn.com/gigcx-discussion-featuring-mckinsey-livexchange-and-newage-products

The text in this appendix is a summarized version of the podcast discussion and was featured in Intelligent Sourcing magazine on August 13, 2021. The original article was written by Mark Hillary.

www.intelligentsourcing.net/gig-cx-debate-who-is-really-using-the-gig-economy-in-cx-and-why/

THE GIGCX DISCUSSION

In the past year, Peter Ryan and I have turned down at least three serious offers to sponsor our podcast, the CX Files. This isn't because we are so wealthy that we can afford to turn away business, it's just that CX Files has gradually grown into one of the most popular CX podcasts in the world and it is 100% independent – there is no corporate sponsor or backer telling us who to feature.

We have always tried to feature genuinely diverse voices from the analyst community, the CX specialists and BPO companies, as well as tech voices and the companies that buy all these services – see recent episodes where we have a telco and health insurance company speaking. We like being able to spotlight any interesting voices without demanding that they pay to feature on the show.

We usually focus on a single voice in each episode, but I recently tried an experiment where the episode focused on **Gig CX**. I wanted to try getting voices from all sides of the discussion onto a single podcast that could stay under 30 minutes.

The Gig CX episode featured three speakers:

- **Vinay Gupta**, Senior Expert, **McKinsey & Company**
- **Mahesh Raghuram**, Director of Customer Service, **NewAge Products**
- **Terry Rybolt**, Chief Revenue Officer, **LiveXchange**

To give some context, Terry's company offers a Gig CX platform that allows companies to quickly build and staff a virtual contact center. Mahesh's company sells garden/garage furniture and equipment (in Canada) and they have often struggled to manage their customer service processes in peak periods – in 2020 they started using Gig CX. Vinay is a US-based management consultant who advises on many emerging trends, including Gig CX.

On one podcast we had a Gig CX platform provider, a user of Gig CX, and a management adviser who knows all about how Gig CX should work. So what did they say?

Mahesh explained what drew his company to a Gig CX model in the first place. He said: "We are an e-commerce company with a high average order value, which means we have massive seasonal peaks. If you if you look at a Black Friday timeframe, or the start of summer, many companies like ours are struggling to maintain their service. You could be waiting 30-60 minutes on a call."

Terry mentioned that the marketplace is learning about Gig CX quickly. He said: "There's around 57 million gig workers in the US alone today – that's data from the Bureau of Labor Statistics. So the gig economy is here, we're now just introducing it into the customer experience environment at scale. This is an educational process – just like it was with work-from-home, we're now educating the marketplace."

Listening to both Terry and Mahesh it was clear that the fear some companies have when they hear 'gig economy' is a lack of control, an inability to manage the quality of interactions, and the sense that the Gig CX workers will take over any existing customer service processes – in-house or those outsourced to a Business Process Outsourcing company (BPO).

In fact, any existing operation can remain as the 'core' with Gig CX layered on top to build more flexibility into the service. I asked Mahesh how complex it was to integrate Gig CX into his existing processes. He said: "It was fairly simple. It just layered in perfectly on top of our existing contact center model. And we were able to get it up and running in about two to three weeks."

He added: "We were definitely looking to launch for Black Friday 2020, because we were so focused on our customer experience during that timeframe. This is the biggest time of our year and we wanted to get it done. We actually reported well over satisfactory service levels throughout our peak season – we were answering calls in under 45 seconds from November all the way to the end of January."

Mahesh has augmented his existing customer service team with a Gig CX team to build more flexibility into the process, but I asked Vinay if this is something the BPO community also needs to consider. How can the contact center experts sell flexibility if they are not also exploring a gig model?

He said: "If we take a step back, Gig CX is all about meeting the needs of the customers. It's not just for in-house teams or BPOs to build this flexibility. There could be multiple ways of achieving the right solution. It could be like Mahesh, with an in-house team also using Gig CX to add flexibility, but I could also ask my BPO partners to add the same flexibility. From a BPO point of view, given this market is going to be very mature very soon. They need to ramp up their capability. If I'm a BPO, and I don't have a flexible workforce, then clients may just find another BPO."

Vinay was clearly suggesting that Gig CX can offer customer service flexibility whether you are using an in-house solution or a BPO. The BPOs that ignore this option may struggle to actually be flexible enough.

Vinay suggested that the key for any manager thinking about Gig CX is to understand how variable the demand for their CX team really is. He said: "I advise my clients that they really understand what kind of variability they are dealing with. Variability comes in different forms. Monday looks different to Friday. You can have different days of the month that are busy. You need to understand this variability and the type of calls that are driving the variability."

As Vinay described this need to plan for variable customer service volumes he mentioned that this variable environment offers opportunities to both companies planning their customer service levels and the agents answering calls. Accepting and managing this variability means that agents can split shifts and work much more flexible hours. This allows companies to reduce hours when volumes are lower and ramp up their team when they know it will be busy. This flexibility is great for people who want more control over their working hours and the companies that don't want a lot of people working during quiet periods. A real win-win for both.

This debate featured three knowledgable voices exploring why and how Gig CX matters for everyone in modern CX. Whether you are managing an in-house customer service operation or a BPO, Gig CX is not about to replace you, but it could help your team to be much more flexible.

Please leave a review on Amazon-it helps more readers to find this book and this will educate more people globally on the opportunities for Gig CX.

Before you go, why not download 'Gig CX: Customer Service In The Twenty-First Century' by the same authors... **http://j.mp/gigcx**

Don't Fear The Gig Worker:
GigCX And The Employment Reboot

Published by LiveXchange Books
Arroyo Grande, California

https://livexchange.com

Made in the USA
Middletown, DE
08 March 2022

62292561R00129